PATTERN EVIDENCE

Pattern Evidence is evidence in which the shape or distribution of a substance provides information rather than the substance itself

PATTERN EVIDENCE

POEMS

Michael D. Riley

RESOURCE *Publications* • Eugene, Oregon

PATTERN EVIDENCE
Poems

Copyright © 2019 Michael D. Riley. All rights reserved. Except for brief quotations in critical publications or reviews, no part of this book may be reproduced in any manner without prior written permission from the publisher. Write: Permissions, Wipf and Stock Publishers, 199 W. 8th Ave., Suite 3, Eugene, OR 97401.

Resource Publications
An Imprint of Wipf and Stock Publishers
199 W. 8th Ave., Suite 3
Eugene, OR 97401

www.wipfandstock.com

PAPERBACK ISBN: 978-1-5326-7904-9
HARDCOVER ISBN: 978-1-5326-7905-6
EBOOK ISBN: 978-1-5326-7906-3

Manufactured in the U.S.A. AUGUST 1, 2019

For all the usual suspects especially
those under protective custody

"Our desire has no remedy."
—St. Teresa of Avila

"This is how one grows: by being defeated, decisively, by constantly greater beings."
—Rainer Maria Rilke

Contents

Acknowledgments | xi

PROBATIVE EVIDENCE | 1
At the Carnival | 3
Summons | 4
Incarnations | 6
Ordination | 7
Metamorphosis | 9

WITNESSES: LOCARD'S EXCHANGE PRINCIPLE | 11
Alone | 13
Welcome | 14
Hello | 15
For My Doppelganger | 16
Two Women | 17
Otzi | 18
Elephants | 19
Lions | 21
Greek Fisherman's Cap | 22
Dimp | 24
The Genius | 26
Seven-Eleven | 28
Work: A Rendering | 30
Chiaroscuro | 31
One Round | 33

Initial Inventory | 34
Tom Disch: In Memoriam | 37
The Sailor's Hornpipe | 38
Bearings | 39
Tommy: A Little Golden Book | 40
Last Walk with My Dog | 44
Aging | 45
Brief Trip | 46
Evening | 47
All Night Diner | 48

IMPRESSION EVIDENCE | 51
Empiricists | 53
Her Name | 54
Up the Stairs | 55
On Mother's Day, For Anne | 57
Praxis | 58
Regular Exercise | 60
Hepatitis C | 62
Why I Love My Driveway | 63
Molly's Arrival | 65
Watching Molly Sleep | 66
Light: For Molly | 67
Molly Knows | 68

Contents

Married | 69
On the Anniversary of My Mother's Death | 70
Love Letters | 71
The Only Wealth | 72
Equations | 73
St. Valentine's Day | 74
Swift Retribution | 76

Background Controls | 79
Map | 81
Beside the Deep Woods | 82
Grackles | 84
Walking | 85
Spring Water | 86
Rain at Dawn | 87
Hunter Gatherer | 88
The Perfect Spring | 89
Wren | 90
Yellow Eye | 91
August | 92
Winter Weeds | 93
Full Moon Among the Sycamores | 94
Hard Rain | 95
Flurry | 96
Snow Tropes | 97
A Winter's Tale | 98
Night Driving | 99
Hard Winter | 100

Composite Drawings | 103
Encounter | 105
Creation | 106
October Field Corn | 107

Monet's Chickadee | 108
"My Egypt" | 109
Breughel's Hunters Return | 111
Model | 113
The Emperor's Clothes: For Sylvia | 115
Spirit Levels | 116
Cultural Exchange | 118
Poetry at Hayfield House | 119
Primary Colors | 120
Urban Muse | 122
Film Noir | 123
Packet | 124
One on One | 125
Figure Skating | 127
Melanoma | 128
Vases | 130
The Calling | 131
Song | 132

Alternative Light Sources | 133
In Crete | 135
Easter Island | 136
Blessing Way | 137
Piercings | 138
The Shaman's Apprentice | 139
Sunday Afternoon, Kinzer, PA | 141
Promises | 143
Chalice and Madonna | 144
In the Name of the Rose | 146
Frankincense | 147
Inheritance | 148

Contents

Money | 149
The Offices of Lust | 150
The Wages | 151
Remorse | 153
In Praise of the Soul | 154
Leafmeal, or
Herb-of-Grace | 155
Children's Night Prayer | 156

ANALYTICAL DRIFT | 157

Awakenings | 159
In Praise of Reading | 160
Dialectic | 161
Digital | 162
You Could Look (It) Up | 163
Apple | 164
At Bay | 165
Calibration | 166
Precincts | 167
Syllogism | 168
Race | 169
Momentary | 170
Tears | 171
Nostalgia | 172

Equanimity | 173
Opticals | 174
Optimism | 175

CLOSE SURVEILLANCE:
EXPERT WITNESS | 177

Zeno's Progress | 179
First Things | 181
Ascent | 182
Joss Stick | 183
Out Like a Lion | 184
Murdering Grandma | 185
Scouts | 188
Grandma Meets Anubis | 189
Dolls | 192
Witness | 193
Kissing the Dead in Sleep | 194

DETECTION LIMIT | 195

Stakeout | 197
A Thickened Plot | 199
In Situ | 201
Near Kigali, 1995 | 202
Aubade | 205

Acknowledgments

A number of the poems in this collection had the good fortune to find prior publication. Those initial appearances:

"Walking," *Argestes*; "My Egypt," *ART:MAG*; "The Sailor's Hornpipe," *Arts and Letters*; "Chiaroscuro," *The Atlanta Review*; "Tommy," *The Awakenings Review*; "Watching Molly Sleep," "Molly's Arrival," "Elephants," "Stakeout," *Big Muddy*; "Opticals," *Black Buzzard Review*; "Aubade," "Otzi," *Blue Unicorn*; "The Calling," *Byline*; "Dolls," "Urban Muse," "The Wages," *California Quarterly*; "Packet," *The Cape Rock*; "Ascent," *The Clackamas Review*; "My Doppelganger," *Co/ere*; "You Could Look (It) Up," *The Common Ground Review*; "Sunday at Kinzer, PA," *Cooweescoowee*; "Beside the Deep Woods," "Ordination," "Poetry at Hayfield House," *The Cumberland Poetry Review*; "Children's Night Prayer," "Night Driving," "Light: For Molly," "Spring Water," *Earth's Daughters*; "Map," *EDGZ*; "Brief Trip," *Exit 13*; "At Bay," "Calibration," "Precincts," *The Fiddlehead*; "At the Carnival," *The Freshwater Review*; "Dimp," *The Front Range Review*; "Film Noir," *The Great River Review*; "On Valentine's Day," *The Green Hills Literary Lantern*; "7-11," *Home Planet News*; "Kissing the Dead in Sleep," "Chalice and Madonna," *Interim*; "In Praise of Reading," *In the West of Ireland*; "Alone," *Iodine Poetry Review*; "Winter Weeds," *Jeopardy Magazine*; "Song," "Cultural Exchange," Kalyna Language Press; "One on One," *The Kerf*; "Equations," *The Ledge*; "Syllogism," *Limestone*; "Grackles," "The Race," "Welcome," *The Lyric*; "Full Moon Among the Sycamores," *The MacGuffin*; "Snow Tropes," *The Mankato Poetry Review*; "Equanimity," *Minimus*; "Monet's Chickadee," *Miramar*; "Work: A Rendering," "Lions," *MUSE*; "A Winter's Tale," "Love Letters," *Nebo*; "Zeno's Progress," "Hunter Gatherer," "The Perfect Spring," "Why I Love My Driveway," *Off the Coast*; "Her Name," "In Praise of Mystery," *Orbis* (UK); "Vases," *Oxalis*; "One Round," *Paper Street*; "Melanoma," "Nostalgia," *Parting Gifts*; "Leafmeal, or Herb-of-Grace," *The Plains Poetry*

ACKNOWLEDGMENTS

Journal; "Empiricists," *Poetry Ireland Review*; "This Is Just To Say," *Poultry: A Magazine of Voice* (Parodies); "August," *The Prairie Wolf Press Review*; "Metamorphosis," *Presence*; "Hepatitis C," *Rattle*; "Regular Exercise," *The Rockhurst Review*; "Last Walk With My Dog," *The St. Andrews Review*; "Initial Inventory," *The Schuylkill Valley Journal of the Arts*; "Creation," "October Field Corn," *Sculptural Pursuit*; "Praxis," *Slant*; "On the Line," *The Small Pond Magazine of Literature*; "Up the Stairs," *The South Carolina Review*; "Hello," *Steam Ticket*; "Blessing Way," *Studio* (Australia); "On the Anniversary of My Mother's Death," *Third Wednesday*, "A Thickened Plot," "The Offices of Lust," *Visions: International*; "On Mother's Day: For Annie," *Wavelengths*; "All Night Diner," *Westview*; "In Crete," *Wings*; "Awakenings," "Wren," *The Worcester Review* (Canada). "Easter Island" is from my *Players*, published by Turning Point.

Probative Evidence

*possesses the potential to provide details
that are valuable to an investigation*

At the Carnival

Behind us
the alligator ride
 rounds

with toddlers,
wide eyes
above

bobbing
plastic necks.

Wondering
what pleasure is.
And fear.
Tears overtake one
in ringlets,

glee the boy
in creepers and stains.

Round and round
they plumb and sound,

wordless
in their tiny seats,

grinning green
crocodiles

front and back,

pulses in quick
circles, bodies

tricked already,
living early

on each nerve.

Summons

Light through the Irish lace
tablecloth dapples the boy
inside the general snowstorm of
brilliance he sits among.

The single window spills
late afternoon all over him,
hidden beside lion legs with
brass tips, mahogany

joists above his head.
'Leg' and 'foot': words of wood,
too, as he runs his hands
up and down their smooth sides.

In the dazzle of freckled light
forehead to sneakers, he changes.
Here and there above his head light
catches dust enough

to make tiny searchlights. He
pinches the lace windows
shut one by one. Each yawns
with light again.

He creeps further, into darkness at
last. He watches the whole hour it
takes for the window to graduate
from flesh to vermillion.

He cannot name the steps
of color, the sealing of their bond with
him in their disappearing.
He holds the grooved mahogany

as if touch were the color he
cannot see outside
the pull of memory. He falls into the
sleepless dream.

Incarnations

Under grapevines and a copper sky he
pushes toy trucks through a world of
his own making, afternoon curled at
his feet, full of industry

behind the little steering wheels he
turns through the squeals
of slashed pigs and sledge-hammered cattle rising
from the slaughterhouse past the fence.

Men in waxed-cotton aprons wave
bloody gloves or bare hands.
Grapes sway on their vines, the sun ripening
outside the ripened cave.

Salt smells, the furring of flies
through the air, a wide-toothed saw
against the bone, marbled hues
where the sun slips past the chimneys.

Beetles flee his deepening roads,
vines of dust looping between grapevine
shadows as he pushes toward
the metal gate and chain-link fence

whose porous boundary soon fills with
reddening twilight, his own face
flushed and tired as the joints on poles sway
steaming past him as they process

to the small butcher shop next door, his
tiny fleet stalled in the dirt blowing
around crushed grapes, the smells of supper in
his head, the houselights glowing.

Ordination

Vestry silk, purple featherings
between pages skinned with color,
etched with flagged capitals, sheet
of caught light over ink.

Pages still alive, heavy
and graceful in turning,
Latin at home among
brown edges, calligraphic flights,

dusk, candlelight wavering
like water, hushed strokes
probing the quiet with text,
curves wet with ideas

older than speech.
Only skin can illuminate,
outlast death long enough to
be read.

Old Latinates
still salty with incense
and beeswax-hardened round
windows, beads of witness

clinging to the syllables.
Investiture. Ordination. Peaked
as the vestry windows latticed
with lead.

When I was young I flew
to the margins where the monks
told vernacular truths:
"My hand is weary."

"Sunlight falls on these knuckles whiter
than the moon."
"Listen! The blackbird calls!"
The page where the smug rat

outruns the cat forever. Now I
scale cell walls mistaken for
limit.
Liturgy, demarcation

straight into chant
down aisles strait with cold
cattails of air around
our ankles, chastened into

unison and plainsong,
watery vowels lapping the stone
corridors with a sound we learn to
pronounce slowly because

its formal life lives so close
to silence.

Metamorphosis

Brutish and short, on my spindly legs
I spin through dust, over harboring walls and
rotting apples. I am the author
of this infinitely sad comedy.

No wonder I frighten the horses, sensible
houyhnhnms trotting the streets
rhythmically as poems, bearing
the load, traveling the mitred paths.

Let the insects come to me,
I said, and soon the little holy cards
appeared everywhere, lithographed in four colors.

I arose against my will in my neat suit and
wing collar, arms extended
to welcome them, the tiniest excuse
for a smile beneath my trimmed mustache.

Come to me, all you who are burdened.
I will tell the true stories of your hunger
to be men. Stretch out your segmented arms and
legs. With your strong jaws
eat the air around you, then fill it again with
words no one understands.

Love calls you to this, and when your
exoskeleton is translucent dust, a
weightless onionskin,
they will sweep you out of the tomb

  into the threatening dawn. Light grows
  among the tombs. Catch it with your emptiness. Wind
  plucks your feelers as it rises,
  shivers them. Now let it lift you up,

shining in the red light, hovering wingless.
Love calls you to this, too, and three days
are not so long to watch and wait.

Witnesses:
Locard's Exchange Principle

is the theory that every person who enters or exits an area
will deposit or remove evidence from the scene

Alone

Among her clothes
she finds another stranger,
held by a sleeve too snug,
ringed fingers
drumming the bar,
quick eyes searching
doorways and melting ice, a
collar fluted with lace
from which her dress travels down, the
skirt angling from her knee crimped in
tight folds
against her chair.

I will find a wrinkle there
as she gathers herself to leave,
slipping her small foot
against the heel of the red shoe
dangling rhythmically
beneath her stool.

As she goes I will guess the
rest: the wise body pressed
against her dress, and all our
loneliness.

Welcome

Quickly she slid into this womb of tears,
Creased and surly, red with woe,
This tiny cork unstoppered from the bloody sea
Of dreams, the soft paddlings of thought,
Its helmet of skin and sealed eyes, Its
umbilical thumb studying peace.

Now the weightless meditation ends
Down the trapdoor of earth, the sack of repose Spilt
down the sides of a rusting kitchen chair Onto tiles
chipped like teeth, where the cat bends Her back up
in wonder, then calmly stares
Into the weeping mess as if to say

Idea's paw prints go quieter than this. I
will go and circle the circling fish.

Hello

She sits her intricate machinery
across the aisle. One knee hooks the other
and rocks the hooked knee's foot through space.

She glories in her density: rhythmic heel,
adjacent knee, upright spine enclosed
by her body's clothes and cardinal appointments

hat to shoes. Her circuitries of face glow
with subtle filigrees, pale sand to peach.
Brow to lip, hydraulically, she pulls me

into wheels of eyes electric blue. I take
her celebration in, forget for once to adumbrate.
The complete history of intention

rides at ease along her hips. All expression
builds a home above the smile crimping her
eye toward me to harness

physicality in some better winch
than gravity resisting face to face
our welcome rising over risk and hills

of nylon luggage, to turn our separate crowds of
one into a something less like two.

For My Doppelganger

How do your ankles hold you up?
They are finger-thin
and you no wider than a wrist.

Buttock to calf seems merely half
the usual allotment.

Were you born for a small efficiency?
Eat-in kitchen, Murphy bed,
paper-thin walls where you would be
the shadow.

If you were a word
you would be already said, a
lovely gift to air and ear.
I love finding you
almost here.

Two Women

Love, he said, the anorect, spare, and strange,
The unplumbed and shifty. Rearrange
The lemons, savor your dates. Worlds on stilts Walk
away in every case and hope wilts
Even in sunshine, shrinking back like skin.
Water it with stealth: Two women talking
Over shopping bags of Schopenhauer.
Their scarves are paisley, their faces dour. Trace
in their hearts the faintest echoing
Of glory overheard on the bus this morning.
Imagine them home. Smell the roast beef steaming,
Soon you will mistake supper for dreaming.
    Lay your head on their antimacassar. Do
    not talk anymore. Do not wonder.

Otzi

His life was so small and still, he despaired
finding it in time. It seemed the rag
of an old shirt, the colors bleached, a
plaid flannel work shirt, valueless
except to patch something else.

Unless Otzi wore it, he thought,
frozen intact in the Alps 5000 years ago, a
marvel now on a par with the pyramids.
Everything: arrows and quiver, some still
un-feathered, straw in his fur boots for warmth,

a pouch with a bone needle and dried meat,
tattoos in three-line groups all over his body
with a ritual significance no one knows.
One murdered man frozen long enough, ice
particles molecularly bonding

capillary to vein, bluing his extremities,
sacrificing everything to save
the surrounded heart, the set of his jaw
hopeless in the storm and arrows
yet so calmed by the clarity of his fate,

he slept on, invaluable, in rigid peace.

Elephants

Smoke-thin and pale
as if the menthol cigarettes

she pulled so fiercely
into herself

froze her simmerings and
escaped

as winter breath,
one snow-blonde cylinder

wound tighter than
the filters she bites down on.

So she collected
elephants

from around
the world,

placid inverted
pears, huge beasts

made small,
decorative and still.

White porcelain
tipped with gold,

a glass ruby
on his headdress.

African ebony
herringboned for skin.

Burled mahogany
trunk to tail.

All through the house
they herd quietly

together, their skin between
the house plant

eucalyptus where
pale bones can rest

and be remembered:
family grounds.

They fear nothing.
Hate nothing. Forget

nothing. They forgive
drought and monsoon,

calves orphaned
and adopted.

Born for worlds
half a world away,

they live here with her,
far below Kilimanjaro's

smoke and ice and ash,
keeping even the lions

and circling scavengers
just far enough away.

Lions

This ferocity will not cease. The slow
sun sinks. They lounge in the pampas grass gorged,
blood-flecked, weary of satieties.
They watch the carrion-birds grow
bold among the ribs. Strings of white muscle
loop one beak. Gory talons dance among wings
like broken umbrellas in a song
of dust. The lions' hooded eyes reveal only
hunger's death and the grip of sleep. Soon
only the humming flies will cripple silence
and fill the lions' dreams with pale urgent
shadows moving through the steep
> grass forever, blood scent seeking always flesh
> not to feed flesh, but take it away.

Greek Fisherman's Cap

I saw it in a *New Yorker* ad
($32 in black, navy, gray or brown,
85% wool, 15% nylon).
The model looked exactly like my old Dean, Ted
Paige, 15 years before he died.

I doubt he owned a Greek fisherman's cap, favoring
the muted style of middle management with less
ugly ties. No doubt he had a frisk
now and then, a Mets cap or yellow windbreaker.
He didn't frisk when I knew him, just ground on.

I like him in this Greek fisherman's cap
and wish now I had surprised him with one. He
still looks a bit silly, as he always did,
assertively uncertain, a boy in a man's shirt.
But the cap helps somehow (hats often do),

gives him a rakish piquancy, a persona.
Ted slid through whatever we thought about him. He
acted. He spoke. Others responded,
often in life-changing ways. Yet, by some quirk, it
was as if nothing ever happened.

In the Greek fisherman's cap, however, he is
an undistinguished man in a Greek fisherman's cap, a
tiny figure in a national magazine.
He could be any one of us, really, anyone with
$32, a plain affect, and a profile

whose Adam's apple no longer elevators so
self-consciously, whose stammerings and
humorlessness and angry self-doubts, against
which he sailed bravely every day,
have become boldly weathered achievements

with muscled forearms and the stink of halibut,
Anthony Quinn dancing alone on the sand to
the theme song. My God, how he danced
while the wreck of it all clattered down the hill. Zorba
himself, the human spirit, deathless Greece.

 He was all of this, his hat would say,
and we would believe it, because we always wanted a
Greek fisherman's cap of our own
to wear as we watch the sluice collapse, hearing
nothing but the dancing balalaika

above our own rapt dancing, to a folk rhythm
we learned without knowing when or how but
have always known, all beneath *our* cap, its
ridiculous jaunty promise held tight
now by the brim, and slapped against our hips.

Dimp

In the full strangeness of 99
he stands before another biplane, a
picture for the Seniors Page.
His bold features seem carved from soapstone.
Except for the words surrounding him
on the page, all he holds of his remarkable life is
another photograph: he and two cronies beside
his first Flying Jenny, the one he flew the bravest
locals in, out of hayfields
and meadows where even the cows looked up.

Before he flew off to his first of two
world wars, the airlifts he directed later,
much later, after he helped get Transcontinental (TWA
long since) off the ground,
conferring weekly with Rickenbacker,
Earhart, and Lindbergh-when Transcontinental
was called Lindbergh Airline in the papers.

His memory of particulars grows dim, the
reporter reports, but the medals keep their
specific gravity well enough
in their velvet cases despite some fading
of the campaign ribbons. Of Earhart he says, "She
flew over so much water, too much water." The
local airfield once called Dimp Field,
his nickname, has long since picked up the
name of the nearest small town, white with
the same cement as all the rest without the
groundhog holes and gullies he steered
around, bucking himself aloft
on his motorized kite, rattling and humming the
miracle until it drowned out
everything but blood and disbelief,
rising again, of itself through him,
and year after year he claimed death
no price at all to pay for it.

He will be there forever, I understood, squinting
in the sun, standing in the cockpit, one hand on
a guy wire, the other
pointing toward the sky, his grin the horizon
caught just at the apex, in a barrel roll,
if a barrel roll could pause and see itself.

The Genius

There's always room for one more like him
except at his own table, where Grandma
purses her lips, narrows her froggy eyes
behind those thick lenses, and stops chasing
peas across her plate to look up with that
outraged sorrow she loved.

Where the kids were dying to whine
if they could get away with it, but instead
wrap their feet around their chair legs and
squeeze their hips from side to side,
constipated-seeming dances to avoid
stillness, silence, meat loaf again, him.

The collie, Quarx, sprawls absurdly under
the table, each leg spread wide, a hairy
compass, a small shag rug sleeping deep
inside that pure dog consciousness
untroubled by Heidegger or split
infinitives, the mystical fog
of being purely in this-moment absconded
by dog dreams even farther from the
impurities of those holding forks.

His wife stares intently at her coleslaw.
She cannot not listen. They belong to one
another, primitive cleansing rituals notwithstanding. He
speaks, and speaks. Oh, DNA, she thinks,
how ill we serve your helix-heart.
Oh, Jesus, when they went to throw you from
that cliff, your home-town neighbors who
raspberried everything you said,
why couldn't they have thrown me instead?

I too am well-acquainted with failing,
he said, smiling with pain as his Cherry Garcia
electrified his pulpy gums. I remember the time before
the time you remember, my dear, before chemistry
ruled the world, and particles and waves, long before
the dinosaurs invented the eon,
even before the faintest idea could construct itself
into semi-articulate fear and awe.

Those were the days, my dear, my dear, my dear, he
said in rhythm to the spoon scraping
the glaze of his bowl, parting the pink melt as
Moses parted the waves-though smaller by a
lot. Let's invent or reinvent something after the
dishes, Maude, something smaller than a
breadbox (remember those?) with no
moving parts at all but which will move nonetheless,
and cry out, and have its being in the heart.

In the heart where everything lives fully,
becoming what it must be on pain of
disappearing, of accepting the nothing that
is for the nothing that must be.
Right here, Maude, in our humble rancher.
We can call it . . . Well, we'll think of something
before the redware dries and the evening news begins.

Seven-Eleven

The gangsters at the mini-mart
sneer and pose, hang danger from
their golden earrings,
flex biceps round with baby fat.

They ogle pink plastic flesh
on the videocassette rack,
grab their crotches and whistle
before the slick covers
of the girlie mags.

Marlboros lit, dangling,
they stab ash toward the floor,
their props perfect: oversized shoes, tattoos,
gang patches on leather sleeves.

"What it means!" one shouts
from the football pages, holding up
a photo of a helmet to the chin, the
receiver's head snapped back like a
bottle cap.

Another rubs his nose and winks,
gestures behind the young girl
buying bread and milk.
A stare from the counterman
turns him, mouth and eyes wide
with fake surprise, swiveling
his hips.

Outside, fluorescent light
burns the padded shoulders of
their black jackets
as they strut, punch
pantomime and laugh.

To be is to be on.
Their white leather high-tops
glow against the asphalt, each
step repeated inside
puddles skimmed by moonlight and
blowing trash.

Work: A Rendering

Glossy bones every morning. Moist
tendon, agon and protagon.
Miles of capillary and vein
surging pints through the first chutes,
industry of picking up, sloughing off,
first snapshots, then the slapping
35 mm hum of memory, he and his father in
thick black boots, waxed cotton smocks,
windbreakers lined with wool and wool gloves, sunlight
glancing off the sloped roof
blinding the factory windows but not dimming
the roaring of the cattle as the shift changes
streamed in and out,
wind cut from the river over knit caps
and lunch pails swung in time to a whistle
chasing sparrows from the eaves
and night from the curbs and hollows
of the street still blood-red with the dawn.

Chiaroscuro

He preferred the black and white wars.
Tanks in mud or snow, soldiers smoking, a
few horses. Fat black limos
gliding down runways, a tiny flag
on each fender, nickel hubcaps gleaming.

Biplanes were even better: kites with guns.
And old film out of time so the men
in flat tin helmets seemed jointed
wooden toys lurching from their trenches.
These were Hollywood's Golden Era.

The big-budget Technicolor epics
left him cold. Once the grizzled corpses
of Pork Chop Hill, the snub-nosed Migs,
gave way to orange napalm clouds blooming in
Disney green jungles, he lost interest.

Too much was lost when he could see that
the body bag was green. He grew up with
The Ten Commandments, Quo Vadis,
The Big Top, and *Carousel.* Give me *Casablanca,*
he'd say, and the Harold Lloyd two reelers.

Those simple shades were magic.
Infinite gradations of the same thing.
You knew, felt, everything, saw everything
but color. The world was truer for the absence. Framed.
Sketched by a perfect pencil. Complete.

Found wanting, the image found itself.
So vigorous a lie must be true
and he knew it now, in his dark room black
and white himself in the thrown shadows of
his old Philco. The profound

is simple, he said, flickering with them
onto Guadalcanal, bobbing stiffly in the water,
his face as gray as theirs in the shells
of flashing light, the waves of blackness.
This far and no farther, he said with Churchill.

One Round

We embrace the bullet, too,
its rifling skewed, bone-splintered
in exiting. And the reflecting pool
of blood, dark as beets,
the strawberry jam of matted hair, eyes
glazed in a dream too profound for
mistakes of caliber and light

or blue-black clouds cornering
days against brick and asphalt,
mercury fuses glowing mutely
into cars without wheels, full of trash. His
gaze takes aim at all this,
could the reflection, its tilt and round
angle of vision, be perfectly spiraled.

Initial Inventory

—in memory of Kit Yeager

All the provisions of her neat Cape Cod,
and the house itself—its ivied borders,
wallpapered and real, one plucked so carefully
from beds at Funk's Nursery, the other no less so
from the wallpaper books lining Carpet Mart
like illuminated manuscripts at Columba's monastery.
Williamsburg blue, taupe, and cream trimmed and
cut in, shaded by subtle degrees
at Home Depot, put on through sweat, gnats,
weekends. Artistic Country she always called it.
Two empty cases of Yuengling Lager returnables
on the porch by the wall.
The John Deere bought on sale and pushed May through
October. The garage filled with Sears shovels, trowels,
hedge-trimmers. The weedwhacker,
snowblower, toolbox full of Craftsman drivers, snippers,
wrenches, all the rest. Rakes, hoes, watercans hanging from
the hookboard. Bags of peat, jars of weedkiller, their
plastic tubes and pneumatic sprayers.

The midsize Chevy coupe whose metalflake
green paint she waited three extra months for.
Her CDs—light rock, New Age, retro oldies and
the surprises like *Missa Luba*,
selections from Mahler, *The Mikado*.
The souvenir plastic waste-bag from Atlantic City
where she loved to gamble and usually won, travel
coffee mug with St. Peter's School
printed on the side, a fundraiser for Girl Scouts.
Stickers from Penn State and Catholic High, sun-
faded, the kids' graduations long since filed away
into blurred and tilted photographs. Three
parking stickers from Kunzler Meats lining the
center top of the front windshield

for the times George had to use her car,
two out of date, one partly peeled away.
A sweater vest forgotten in the trunk.

Inside, exponential leaps of choice
and personality. Kix, Wheaties, Liquid Plumbr, Comet
instead of Ajax, dishes in Pfaltzgraff's Wheat pattern
and juice glasses once filled with soft cheese. Hundreds
of decisions in the kitchen alone.

Closets full of insights for each season,
lined with dozens of parallel shoes,
loafers, sneakers, heels in their shoeboxes.
Drawers of lingerie, jewelry, and socks.
Shaker style cherry furniture paid off in installments,
their drawers full of photos that never found
their books, waiting to be reborn with light.
More Williamsburg greens, blues, and brick reds,
period wallpaper of old samplers, lives repeated
all over the walls. Her expert stenciling and embroidery
framed and hung. Two watercolor landscapes—
quite good—from her evening classes at Harrisburg Area
Community College ("HACK" for short, of course).
Books and more CDs, pills in the medicine chest in
childproof plastic multiples, boxes
in the attic full of her own childhood,
nearer boxes in the basement waiting
for yard sales and Goodwill. Holiday lights
and decorations for every season:
pumpkins, shamrocks, strings of tiny red hearts, a
whole wall of Christmas cartons: balls, lights, two
outside reindeer, her specially-cushioned Santa and
angel collections.

So bare every beginning. The bones
would not be sturdy enough even if
the rest of the cereals were named, the perfume bottles
on the dresser, their exact amounts

to the milliliter, and better analogies than
the names for their scents: Jungle Fruit,
Sunset Hibiscus, Citrus Sun Musk.
Exact dates, hours, minutes, seconds, nanoseconds.
The children's ages, their every quirk along
with every second of their histories. Those
of everyone else she ever knew.
Her word billions lost in air, or in her own
synapses, each unarticulated instant
she housed for 51 years, the uncountable store
of a life played out, we all said,
far too soon, only to realize how wrong
we were, that in the end this life collapsed,
like all the other lives she loved,
beneath the weight of its own richness.

Tom Disch: In Memoriam

Tom the trickster is dead,
trap-doored by the .22
beside him on the bed,
a too-large rose beneath his head
and nothing more to rue.

The ended story gets
more compelling every time.
What Tom ran out of sweats
to be born. His new book
waits in stacks and takes all bets.

Tom's tattooed arms
were uncrossed, and that brain that
launched a thousand charms, harms,
alarms has been slain.
He cools. The poems and novels warm.

He'd get the joke right off.
He always did. He copyrighted it.
Now everything's soft
that once was hard. "Abandon shit
you can't scrape off," he said. Or would have.

"He seemed happy, " one friend said.
"For Tom." The new book, his long
grieving coming to an end, or seeming
to. Who can look
close enough? Everything bends.

Tom was radically bent,
and even brilliance can only pretend so
long. Someone told him a .22 would
only dent that skull he rented. Two days
later, off he went.

The Sailor's Hornpipe

The smells of his body rose up as thoughts,
articulate sensation to identify
him to himself, anchors of memory
to tug at the stern and hold back the sails, ropes
groaning in their sockets and wind everywhere.
In the mirror the face
of a sailor considers with seedy curiosity
the overripe clue he looks through

into so many waves of information,
wrinkling moments on the horizon
breaking light into foam. Ship
and ocean, journey and port, he is his
own stale metaphor barely alive
among oil slicks, condoms like rootless
tube worms, a trail of plastic party ware
and one unrolling spool of gauze

rinsing bloody evidence not quite clean
where the rest already sail without him
their yachts, dinghies, tugs, bass boats,
windsurfers tacking bravely on
toward the new world he contracts
before his mirror, into an odor
reminiscent of the sea-smell of sex,
evolutionary perfume blown over the surface,
only odorless darkness miles below.

Bearings

I wore out two teddy bears. This could be
maudlin in other hands (and in my own).
Distinct except for the absence of bone,
the first was pink, soft, shapeless, as tall as me.
Worn to a filthy poverty, he died
overnight and rose next morning as a bear small
and brown, neat in sweater vest, his fur tightly
curled, a plastic snout, and button-eyed.
I have lost the boy, haven't I? As he tried
to do, anthropomorphically shrewd
already, forked unfeathered things to hold against
the dreams of waking, and of sleep.
    I should go back and edit out the fear,
    the preciousness. I can't. The past is here.

Tommy: A Little Golden Book

Even as a very little boy
Tommy ate far too much and
nobody knew why,

least of all Tommy,
who just ate and ate.

I'm always hungry,
Tommy said. Tommy's mother said
he would eat the dog
if he could catch him.

Then Tommy's mother would laugh.
Pass the peanut butter, Tommy said.
Some people thought
Tommy had seen something terrible
when he was very small.

A fox tearing off
a chicken's head.

A burnt little girl
running naked from napalm.
His father hurting his mother.
But he never did,
or not a lot.

Drunken weekends,
long crooked drives
and arguments.

Everyone had those without
eating the wallpaper and
walls, too.

What did all that chewing
have to do with it?

His mother worried

as kitchen chairs groaned
and Tommy got angry and sad.

I made your favorite, she said.

In his teens Tommy watched
movies and TV. A lot.
He read a million magazines
and books.

Like a big sunflower,
Tommy leaned toward the bright,
glowing girls.

Just don't eat so much,
everyone said. You'll be a handsome boy. So

Tommy tried and tried.

Then he ate in bed under the blankets.
By the side of the road
when he learned to drive.
In the bathroom stalls at school.

He hid candy bars all over the house.

What shall we do?
What shall we do? everyone said.
Tommy said it, too.

So the doctor gave Tommy pills to
make him stop eating.
And they did.

And stopped a lot of
other things, too.

And started a lot of
still other things.

But for a few years
Tommy stayed thin
on the outside.

He got married, had two
children, worked hard and
got ahead.

These pills are killing me,
Tommy said one day.
Then he threw them all away.

Slowly then soon
he was eating and eating
more and more.

Tommy got bigger than ever.
And slower. And weaker.

"Is there pizza in heaven?"
Tommy joked to Father Tony.

"New York style thick
with extra pepperoni!"
Then Father Tony laughed.

Tommy "died unexpectedly,"
the paper said. He was
forty-seven years old. He

had eight pallbearers.

Everyone brought the best
they could buy or make
to Tommy's wake:

Beef, ham, turkey, gorgonzola,
Roquefort and brie, macaroni and macaroons,
Scottish shortbread and Kaiser rolls,

deviled eggs and devil's food cake,
whoopie pies and death by chocolate,
chocolate stout and Bailey's Irish Cream.

Tommy's wife smiled a smile
thin and sad, and then she sighed,
"Dear heaven, my Tommy would have cried."

Last Walk with My Dog

Russet leaves dip and soar around
us, rusty scars in the air.
Now and then one slides down Friend's russet fur. His
throat, thick with cancer,
slows us down, makes him wheeze and remember.
He finds me with one backward stare to
learn why the innocent suffer.
Then he scours the ground, augurs
the air with his intelligent nose once more,
his ears forward as his tail stirs the air.
His white paws crush the dead leaves to powder.

Aging

The happy face balloon
tied to the birthday bear
forgets everything.

Fugitive looks back
and forth the air-conditioned currents
he, searching,

sends above the helium
invisibly leaking
until his black smile

forgets his dentures
by the bedside table again.
His eyes tighten over dry tears.

The bear, a stoic, awaits the
complete collapse
of the face he chose to show

the world. His shoulders
tense. He will not look
up. Not yet.

Brief Trip

Back from a two-day overnight I found
the four bananas ripened and one dead mouse.
We couldn't find the live traps anywhere while
the dung and urine claimed the kitchen
counters every morning. Hygiene, of course.
Still, I didn't like it, having gone aground
like a Hindu lately, who once skewered
rodent and spider with the best, or worst.

What other trips am I taking unawares.
With Doris next door, perhaps, who suffers her
Alzheimer's with us because her husband cannot
let go. Yesterday a small gold angel and one
silver salt shaker, both swaddled
in a cat food coupon. "For you," she smiled.

Evening

I can barely hear the field mouse
nibbling at the dog's dish on the kitchen floor two
rooms away,

low alto drumming mantel clock,

Grandma's TV on the third floor
reduced to less than language, its
pitching voices a cello plucked
randomly over a scale.

Another lunge of the oil heater
dims the light for one second,
genuflection before the steady prayer
murmuring now beneath our feet.

Cars slur their vowels
past the window, drunk with
motion and always leaving.

Claws twitching against the hardwood, Mags
dreams in sprints,
herding ancestral sheep.

The thermostat converts the pipes from
cold to hot and back again,

almost in balance.

All Night Diner

Gray formica with darker shadows,
crooked names scratched in crooked hearts.

Silver Deco edges, triple fluting
with silver rivets cling to 1933.

Red leatherette split twice Is
twice spliced by red tape,

two seats curved like airplane wings
fly toward each other forever

over continents of dried gum,
chipped linoleum, crossed ankles in old shoes.

One thick rivet rusted to the floor
yearns for its lost mate and shakes

cups and saucers, ice cubes
and silverware in its derangement.

We sit alone together
under a stainless-steel canopy

curved like a hangar before windows
full of streetlights and rain.

Coffee drips endlessly into
the brown sea we fly over.

From the grille, dawn mist rises.
Cigarette signal flares flicker and die.

Our mirrored doppelganger leans
low over his cup.

Salt. Pepper. Sugar. Glass mugs
half full, held in reserve

before a white flag of napkins.

Impression Evidence

is created when two objects come in contact with enough force to cause an impression

Empiricists

How can we explain to them,
the young, our hypotheses:
lively questionings of arm and wrist,
ankle and tongue, and among
the fine hairs at the nape,
the calibration of nuance
and periodicity of desire
catalogued through long nights of
sleepless observation
when the moon slipped down
the test tube of our window,
all the premises of limbs and lips,
lengthy arguments of flesh
from which deductions of love arise?

They would not believe us.
What have so many nothings to
do with love.

And so the sufferings
will not calm them:
the slow drain of hours
emptied of significance,
all the shabby disguises of self
seen through a microscope, the
shells of dead formulae
on contact paper, a beaker of time
stale with coffee on a sill,
an unmade bed of hopes.

How could they imagine
these uncertainties binding
our facts together,
or know that we have learned
to take for granted more even
than they hunger for?

Her Name

He wants the words to be lovers,
loaves and fish, silhouettes of dead faces. He
loves the dream of language,
who the dream will become next.

His mother knew when she whispered him
asleep, and he slept.
Now he nods on the last Goatstown bus in
a mist of flowery sweet perfume.

He sees her walk away with her head down
through yellow circles of streetlights,
hears the airbrakes sigh, the doors slap shut and
he is left riding, wordless, home

as full of her as the blood that bears
his question above the rhythm of the tires
lulling him to sleep above the name
of every street he travels through.

Up the Stairs

Come up to the flat, she said, her
eyelashes black fans
against her face. I felt the breeze.

We could have a drink, she said, her
tongue glistening in the street light
as the word "drink" caught fire,

then pulled up short for a smile I
counted dumbly tooth by tooth.
Up the stairs I counted, too,

smelling the wet woolen shoulder
of her coat confused by her perfume, heard
the quick knock her heels tacked

down the carpet with, held hard by
the shifting intentions inside her rising coat. We
went together to the door

I counted on, but in the hallway
we joked too soon of love.
She was the woman I dreamed of

through my thirties, but I was forty now.
We teased our other lives from hiding, the
semblances we counted on.

It was too late, so we talked of time,
rectitude, and Proust, sipped wine the
color of hammered gold,

lost and found ourselves between two
theater tickets in a blazer pocket and
two old stories not brief enough

for the evening news, too long for
the middle of the night, a cool
cotton pillow case, and the moon:

that old cat-burglar
climbing the dozing stairway
of city roofs all the way home,

but never quite making his getaway.

On Mother's Day, For Anne

All womb and desire,
shapes set aside
for growth beside banked fires, nights
long with shallow breaths when the
hearth cools
and pain sings in our legs
and sides and hearts.
Together we sway offbalancing
the heavy habitudes we wear, our
linked murmurings:

Gristle, blood, and bone our
cradle, time and space love's
laboring begun.
We swell and bear, our love borne,
and in the bearing, known.

Praxis

—For Annie

Your practical art softens the corners
of this hard house—the draped line of curtains
crewel-stitched, pinch-pleated, the squared black curtain rods you
shopped city and county for, and found.

Wreaths in wheels, brushstrokes of dried flowers
worthy of a Japanese master fishing with a stylus
on waveless seas. Fronds pale as skin
haunt translucent vases. Collisions ring

from the tubular chimes on each porch corner,
harmony from random chances, the wind groomed
for a little domestic night music
to enhance your figurines, backlit and bound

by glass. We are born for decoration. You
love shoes and white ceramic angels. I love
to watch your foot nod to the beat of any
song. Your tiny gold necklaces

hang small, perfect thoughts from your neck. They
collect in the open book of your jewelry box.
Without really trying, you braid
four kinds of evergreen together:

juniper, boxwood, blue spruce, and Norway. One
S-curve of ribbon, cranberry and gold, circles the
lacquered basket where they seem to grow again
from Cleopatra's barque.

What is beauty but hope in love with
everything it finds. I found you
through beauty long before I knew
beauty was practical as a nail,

as necessary as these nothings that never fail.

Regular Exercise

Every one of the 14.4 million skin particles I
lost today mourned on its way
into our carpet, vents, furniture, or yard.
They despaired of touching you.

Although my olfactory labyrinth
can detect 10,000 delineations
of perfume and funk, your Jean Nate and
White Shoulders eclipse them all.

I don't know how many of my 200,000 eye
muscle movements three days ago were
devoted to focusing your flank
or the delights along your wrist bone and calf,
nor how many of my retina's
100 million light receptor cells
ignored the shadows you refused to share, but
they were nowhere near enough.

Anymore than the 48,000 words
I trafficked in that managed to avoid
your name. I waited and waited this morning
for the over 7 million shades of color
these eyes are tuned to see
to resolve into the portrait that perfects them.

The bone marrow that holds up the
bone that holds me up
makes 140,000 blood cells each minute.
They were barely enough two days ago
to turn me in time to follow you out the door,
then lean me toward your departing taxi.

You must forgive the 45 scalp hairs I
lost yesterday because you know
my 104,000 heartbeats—especially the irregular
ones—depend on you for oxygen
and gravity, and each of my 23,000 breaths.
My 60,000 miles of blood vessels
run like Roman roads back to you.

I was supposed to have laughed
an average of 15 times today, but
I fell short. And those three before
your e-mail were rueful
despite your picture among the grandchildren.

No wonder I was tired last night, 17
million brain cells remembering.
17,000 blinks later, each empty of you, and
anyone's eyes would have to close.

I do know that each of the 40 to 70
times I shifted in my sleep three nights ago, I
thanked each unconscious muscle twice for
knowing you were next to me, magnetizing
my 100 trillion cells
toward true north, and busy, I prayed, with
one synaptic billionth's dream of me.

Hepatitis C

It's a new disease, meaning some
microscope found it out ten years ago
and added it to its sisters, A and B, long
renowned for fear and loathing.

It showed up after a needle-stick
Annie suffered at work, but who can tell. It
might have been simmering forty years
from her childhood anemia transfusions.

Here it is anyway, transforming her blood
just enough to be seen. All else is tame. It
might remain so all her life.
Or it might creep. Or rage.

It wears evil's mystery well for so young a
disease: we can't predict it or cure it but
now we know it's here. It loves
the liver and can't wait to take that red meat

down new trails of sacrifice. (Unless, as
I said, it doesn't.) When (if) it starts,
though, it will move by the most
infinitesimal steps: tiny crow's feet

by the eyes, networks of fragile
varicosities on her cheeks, a slowing
step of energy indistinguishable
for months—or years—from aging itself.

The symptoms, in short, are subtle
in the extreme and will require the most
careful attention, or inattention,
the strain of which is identical.

Why I Love My Driveway

Because its proportions soothe the heated corners of
our house. Because this spring two ferns
broke through its rubberized gravel
to stand two feet above their split macadam craters. Because it
curves around the rock garden and crabapple before it
disappears into the garage.
Because the lip of its edge shines so blackly in
the rain it is as if a tongue passed over it.
Because it flows into the busy passing street
like water, speech, vows, imprecations,
but invites privacies sufficient to let
most of them pass by on radial tires and seasons.
Because what I pretend is mine contends with me
every foot of the way, August dust,
autumn leafmeal, February cubits of snow.
Because Annie walks it soundlessly
in her sailcloth sneakers to water
our shared land as far as the hose can reach.
Because her tulips, silver dollars, lupins,
sunflowers, Johnny-jump-ups, and geraniums
glow more brightly above that black line's limit,
and because each spring to cup the blossoms in
your hand and hear the bees, you must walk over
its pebbled tar, held up, affirmed.
Because the smell of hot asphalt
is unforgettable and unique, like the day
the loud, oily crew from Pflumm Brothers
plumbed, poured, steamrolled, and edged a new surface
around us that already needs black rubber sealant
to preserve what we've begun. Because I
must decide between the fern craters
and uniformity. Because I can watch them rise again.
Because the children's feet played here so long
I can still see them scattering after basketballs,
frisbees, batons, and scrawling with chalk

on this blackboard their equations of childhood
waiting for the rain. Because from my upstairs window, I'm
surrounded by a moat I can drown ideas in all day but
which protects me from nothing, not even their return.

Molly's Arrival

Molly did not arrive
until I saw her fingertips.
Holding her was gift enough
at first, her tiny frame shivering,
stretching and curling,
pushing herself up already
at two months, standing on laps,
our hands circling her like a bud vase.
Those big eyes and smiles.
I don't believe in involuntary
muscles today.

She arrived in my weakness, myopia's
microscope, eyeglasses off,
those perfect fingernails impossibly small
right before my eyes.
Straight across as if just clipped,
cuticle the palest shadow,
non-stop in pliant grasping
and unloosing, translucent
in the glow of the table lamp,
knuckle and wrist barely visible as
threadlike creases. But these
manicured creations, like her
luminous eyes, come to us whole.

Detail, like warmth and need,
welds you to us, as you find
in the mystery of your new body
yawns, sneezes, sleep, flexings,
hunger, and cries,
that rush of motion and sound
coming to eye and ear in their unknowable
particularities, embodied souls
grounded beyond endless disguise
too perfect to be explained,
much too perfect to be missed.

Watching Molly Sleep

Cells in growth's controlled riot
swarm through her new life, comprise that
life in its felt foundation—
every infant a synesthete, the world a
glorious sensory tangle.

Turning wrist, shivering fingers,
reverberating voice thrilling her neck
and mouth, pulling her lips back
and the fat tears from her eyes.
Soon enough, she will name those tears and
fail again to hold them in.

Her head tilts, wobbles, the slack spine a
gift now, like the pliable rolls of flesh,
still a soft egg inside the world, shielded
from everything but dreaming,
awake and asleep, the hum of touch and color
teasing open this greater dream.

Light: For Molly

Erin and Molly are safely back
in California. The bedclothes are stacked
by the washer in the basement, the crib we
borrowed at the bed's foot, its ribs repeated
in shadows on the floor.
The stripped bed and crib are the dour color
of ivory, the shade of white in old age.
I will run the vacuum tomorrow, its rage to
remove an almost welcome roar.
In the meantime I retrieve from the floor
beside the bed a green water glass with a
melted inch of ice
playing in the light from the window.
At nine weeks Molly just fit the hollow
of my arm. I walk downstairs with her slight
weight against my chest, into the bright sunshine
from the front door windows.
So very light, and not nearly light enough.

Molly Knows

I hold Molly, who held all of us
last week with hugs, large bright books
with interactive pages, the big dollhouse her
cousin Julie loaned us,
a little plastic world a lot like ours
we could arrange between us.

At eighteen months she is full of both worlds. Words
come in small surprises,
as Pop-Pop did to great applause the
day before she left, but she is full
of other signs, some taught by her mother:
patting her stomach for Help, index finger on
her palm for More, rapidly rolling fingers on
both hands for Mother's Breast,
all the old chestnuts like two arms
upraised for Hold, extended face
and lips for Kiss, her hand around your finger to
take you where she wants to go.

She glories in expressiveness,
runs along all the lines between us, from
the impossible fragility of her neck,
hands, feet, the tiny white cleats of her first teeth in
her broad smiles, her unstoppered bursts
of frequent laughter when she stoops as
if she would implode
without the jest of consciousness.

Married

I consider my fingers, crack my knuckles
then make a fist, wait by the window
for your return from the x-rays.
What are the skeleton, breast, spleen, and lungs minute
by minute but objects of faith
between kisses and visits to the grave? My
mother's urn was brass,
I guess. I know it was shaped like a book I
couldn't read. She lasted seven years once
it decided to move into the bone.
We stood in the cold before a shallow grave next
to my long-dead father's deeper one, letting their
mismatched dust find again
a level we all could live with,
you and I holding hands already.

On the Anniversary of My Mother's Death

The first big winter snow came late.
Early spring had begun to string
her hammocks between our dreamless trees
when this low pressure center roared up from
the South. Reinforced by the Gulf, grown
stronger beside the Atlantic,
isobars tightened steel springs
around our lawns and houses. The snow sandblasted
every windowpane,
wind swayed the pines and savaged the
few tentative leaves just greening
sycamore, elm, and oak. As the howling grew, we
gathered before the fireplace,
watched the recurrent pattern fire threw
above the ceramic logs that never burn, only
blacken, orange darts filling the black center
—small and predictable,
sending us more light than heat.

Love Letters

Carve upon my deciduous heart
Love letters, the whole sharp alphabet Down
deep into the cedar springs of scent
Where the sap pinges the blade, thick and wet
With blood along the edge, filling the wound
With a flood of remembering, a glove
Each contouring atom knows as love
Since the first spring downward toward the ground When
the sky wept and begged, and the dirt loosened Beneath his
fingers, planted in her heart
The idea of seed, then the strict art That
heals the long scar of the seasons.
So the evidence we have grown to crave
Grows past the passing we engrave.

The Only Wealth

Extrapolated souls the only wealth
of sonnets, held up to the surrounding light,
its play of definition rounding
the curvilinear promise of the text.
Come closer, everything says, madness and
love. Roll through the awakening fear
response, outline and detail. From the here
now, over down, the analogic quest
given up on before you realized
her eyes among the others, glowing wild
in lamplight and fever. You are the child
hunger calls itself today, recognized.
> Beside her kitchen stove, be still, listen to
> her stir of voices. Taste each of them.

Equations

I measure the press
Of your lips, light words before sleep,
Your limbs within these rooms
Steep with light, restraining the walls
Where ferns ran like water
Down the window wells.

I calculate the slant
Of sunlight through my heart
And through your hair
Where you slept in the flowered chair
Beneath a hundred roses
Papered on the walls.

I tally and compute
The angles of your face Half
in shadow just above
The sunlit slope of your breast,
Each fractional trace, Exponentials
of loss.

I reconsider the cost
Embracing you in sleep
And memory, the orange cat
Curled away from me upon your lap,
The traffic clashing in the street, Your
hand in fur yellow and deep.

I matriculate the morning
Night after night, resist the slow
Day's decay, still darkening
The paper roses, add you to everything I
see, subtract everywhere I go
The sum of sun from shadow.

St. Valentine's Day

The balloon I bought for her
Banged its empty head against the roof,
Snapping its pink ribbon
Taut above the back seat Where
the roses and mums
Lay banked like a Pasadena float- A
helium heart lighter than air,
An afterthought of youth,
One foot wide in candy-apple gloss, One
side a dove cartooning love, "Happy
Valentine's Day!" on the reverse.

We tied it to a lamp where it could catch the light,
Dance at its ribbon-end, soar and spy
Upon the coffee table where the flowers died.

Except the kids, of course, cut it loose
To watch it bump its head against the ceiling,
Get stuck in corners like an old intention Until
the radiator waves nudged it on again And we
all forgot to pay attention.

Until one night, alone Before
a TV filled with snow
And dozing through another life,
I woke with horror
As its wrinkled form hovered into view,
Heart-high now, its limp finger of ribbon
Writing on the carpet.
It took a labored breath,
Shuddered past the chiffonnier,
Then disappeared.

Now she stalks me everywhere,
This dove doomed by collapsing wings
To skim the unseen currents of our house, As
if I alone could resurrect
The exact branch and curving thorn To
press her dying breast against.

Swift Retribution

What would happen to love
if we woke up one morning in translucent skin?
Guys would still say, "What a pair of lungs!"
but would they also say, "What a capillary web!" or
"Check the curl of those intestines!"

Would we just find in our more visible partner more
to love and hold our interest?
Or would we be distracted mid-kiss
by her intricate sinus cavities—especially
if one were draining, and we could watch
its slow progression to her nose?

How much does love depend upon
imagination anyhow? The fold of nylon
against her hips in the wind,
hints of lace, tiny exclamation points,
tucked fabric a guide for his arms
around her empire waist.
Rouge, mascara, all the rest
to keep the game played in the candlelight of
the mind, all to leap past
these throbbings, choosing the tan, muscled outline
over the busy contents, the slick machinery
holding her up to view.

Spirit insinuating his ghost between her
knees, saving the suckling child
from Mammal World and the mechanics of
the old 35mm flickering black and white on
the wall of the bachelor party,
the groom drunk and staring, comparing.

Sweet trampoline of flesh and bone!
How we pretend to long to cut away
what we kill each other to keep.
How did that rascal Swift put it?

"For, if we take an examination
of what is generally understood by *Happiness,* as
it has respect, either to the understanding or the
senses, we shall find all its properties and
adjuncts will herd under this definition:

That it is the perpetual possession of
being well-deceived." Perpetual!

Let me in there! both sexes say.
I see your uvula convulsing through
protestations of love. I feel you moving
against my knee, your bicyclist's thigh
rigid in my hands. I am lost between your
smile and the fillings in your teeth, randy
for that embrace direct to spirit (with a
little clumsy pleasure in between).

Background Controls

are, typically, samples taken from an area near the target sample

Map

One day all that remains
lies face down in the deep grass,

arms and legs full out,
nose and mouth full bristle and scent,

ears canine to the smallest
rasp each hair of lawn,
tickling, brings,

hands and bare toes
buried to the first
knuckle,

genitals cool and damp,
one last green thought marks the spot.

Dig here, it says.

Beside the Deep Woods

Light dies along each leaf edge,
falls into the deep woods
as shadow, feels its way around husks
of bark, leafdust, nut casings, infinite
thin tangling branches,
one squirrel my gray ghost
between darkness and the light.

Too many greens, this green.
Almost white the sunlit sumac.
Black the nearly hidden pines.
Yellow to lime to olive the garden
in between. Ceaselessly, infinities
of shredded light complicate shape
and surface,
draw what blurs from what does not

as the wind moves in and out,
rearranges each stick of furniture,
opens and closes each window.
Sight denies me boundary, muffles
sound, smell, and touch, so much in
love are these woods with the eye.

One white butterfly weaves at
eye level his chaotic stitch
across his green sea. He moves
forward by every crookedness
wind and instinct can devise:
double backs, steep dives, wide arcs.

His shadow plays beneath him, grows
and shrinks as his white wings, too, go
black with shadow—only to open

again with light,
pulse of limit, or limit's reflection
he leaves behind him as the genius of
this place, the penalty of joy.

Grackles

Strutting and nodding, an early grackle wakens
the rock garden into mid-March sun. He picks
apart the winter thatch: leaf spackle,

dust, branch and needle. His remorseless stiletto
beak tosses leaves over his shoulders, trapping
sunlight inside the oil fire gloss

of wing feather in each thrust. He disables the
debris of silence, come back
on the cusp of a season insatiable

as the old. Last August his shadow swept
down beneath the brimming feeder to crush
a young sparrow in his crow's

feet while pecking out its eyes. It was dead
before we could react. Now he is back,
on the dark imperative he leads

or follows to our yard and that seed milled too
fine for even his relentless will.

Walking

On the road we recognize our feet, hail
each grain nubbing up to meet us,
measure against drifts of cloud
bright-sided barns and houses. Ourselves. Cattle
ignore us perfectly.

A black and white dog tears weeds at
the limit of his chain, pretending they
are us. We delight in distance. In talk
blowing through the air.
We pin on wildflowers for hearts.

We walk into the air two by two,
into a blue frame above hills
lush with honeysuckle, color our boon
companion, context everywhere.
Time and space the only clothes.

Spring Water

The pump clears its throat,
draws a sharp breath as the handle rises, gasps
before the clear stream
rushes down, pneumatic resistance
against my wrist, fingers and palm rust-
flecked, scraped by rust-pimples.

The wide stream, after it coughs
and flushes, flows its mirror down
into the wood-sled bent
with old tin, distorting trees and faces,
too pure for what it looks on.

Put your tongue here, it says.
The word "spring" will chill
your brain with knowledge perfect
as this taste you cannot describe,
only savor and take into yourself.
Bend down now. Begin.

Rain at Dawn

After this rain, earth breathes.
Day rises deftly from its gray bones.
Searchlights of mist probe
dank tunnels of leaves and limbs,
swarming molecules of gold.

Always they appear as qualities of light, these
refreshments and changes,
as our ideas become a matter of words,
condensing and rising again.

Toward this horizon
heavy with uplifting air
we too emerge from the shroud of rain
winding our souls so tightly
in sheets, shy with sleep
but talking already of the night buried
too far away
from this nurturing dream,
first mirrorings of the light.

Hunter Gatherer

I cultivate the insights of my lawn,
root-thick with dirt turning green.
The idealism of elm and maple
uplifted all winter, the persevering
mentality of the sycamore, sacrificing
its skin for wisdom year after year.

I pluck rough syllables of bark
from the elm, knowing it will forgive me
everything. Forsythia has practiced death so
long, spring is pure resurrection
when its gray limbs bloom bitter yellow flags.
I wish I had noticed this years before

rather than the pink sex-cut azaleas,
the ponderous innocence of the tulip trees, white
headlights of pear blossoms sweeping by.
I learned to read slowly. It took a while
to see underground, resolve contradictions
among bud, bare limb, and berry.

It took longer to verify. I dreamed years away before
attempting to cup my palm under
one ripe thought, lift to my nose one insight
sharp as citrus, feel it sink its square root brain
to fingerprint. I had to become that child who
foresaw the sum of his experience.

That's never easy. Luckily for me
what I turned down last year reappears.
Borne down blade and sillow, it will not
ignore each new divide running transverse
through the lower yard, splitting only to
come together, even as I raise my head to wait.

The Perfect Spring

I refuse it on principle,
all feather-fans of dogwood,
azalea so electric pink
your eye jitters, refuses to focus,
but suddenly you understand the Impressionists. I
refuse the wet earth smells,
lime-green new-mown grass
so damp the spears ride your pantleg all
the way to the knee, wrinkles
of lilac filling the windows
with scent while still invisible,
the first silk rags of iris hanging on the fence. All
the old tricks. Sleight of hand.
Another winter up her bathrobe sleeve.
Don't fall for it for once, the bare feet, the
uncinctured waist and crooked smile.

Now if all your dead family and friends had
the same convenient trick
of pulling themselves up from the cemetery,
shamefacedly brushing off their old skin,
scrubbing with a soft brush, ruddying up the
new baby-soft stuff, rinsing their eyes,
flexing stiff new muscles, why, then
there might be something to it. Bringing them
new clothes and that first cold beer.
Catching them up on the winter news,
wars and bestsellers. Getting back to the gym together.
Then you could sit your pints
side by side on the scrubbed porch furniture, look
past the mowed lawn with a smile
as the mailman comes around in his gray
worsted shorts, grins and waves a fistful of
junk mail you suddenly want to read.

Wren

I would choose the wren's day,
first wash of morning, bloom and clear.
Gold leaf evening, when night delays each
edge, then spreads like water.

I would be brisk about it, too, small
and purposeful as a girl playing
house, quick as a piccolo over my
wooden stops and scales.

I will learn to ventriloquize,
surround their house with sound
immanent and rare. For eyes
I will give them ears, newly found.

No matter the event
or weather, joy or grief,
I will keep the covenant
of shadow, song, and leaf.

Yellow Eye

On the hottest day of the year, a
grackle visits the bird bath.
He drinks delicately, extending his
astonishing sleek black body—a
luminescent arrow in flight—
as the water slides down.

It cannot be cool, only necessary.
As he stretches his survival
nearly vertical on the battered edge of
the rim, I consider his yellow eye.
Chinese lacquer-ware
cannot gleam so brightly. The tiny
black pupil says, I am the coldest
thing you will ever see. I perceive and
kill—as I did that sparrow
six years ago just beyond the back steps, pecking
his eyes out in seconds,
before you could open the screen door, screaming
at something beyond
my cold artistry.

Death is beautiful, like my yellow eye. Remember
how at peace that sparrow was without eyes to
see you trembling
or the blood droplets on the sidewalk. He
felt little. He feels nothing now.
I am innocent. That bewilders you
enough to think you hate me. But you
love my death's-head black and sleek efficiency.
You wish the tiny eyes that follow you all
day could be so neatly closed. I see
you standing in the shadow of your door. What
would you give to gain my yellow eye?

August

We grind down to stillness,
suspended thoughts
half alive at the end
of sentences,
mist in motionless pools at
the limits of vision.

Leaves tire at noon
of wind and sun and green, mortal
yellow bruises
on the temples of the trees.

One twirls past windshield
and curb dancing with
precognition.

Children's daydreams unravel.
The space of longing grows.

Cicada shells tighten
on the sycamore, then
split their backs. Souls
take flight.

Air refuses and one by one
the rows of corn lower their flags.

Combines and evening storm
fall as stillborn sounds
into the widening silence.

We do not wait. We linger.

Change begins in the body, along
relaxing nerves, steadying pulse,
surrendering heart to
instinct, harvest, sleep.

Winter Weeds

Thistle and weed,
autumn tweed
a sharp wind

thins
into days, skinned
hours down to these

bright jacket sleeves.
Cold leaves
to bone tomorrow:

snow
piled high
against the marrow.

Full Moon Among the Sycamores

Found out once more by the full moon
Risen among the sycamores,
I find bare limbs the color of the moon Already,
now lit as from within

By the moon again. They glow more naked Than
flesh upon a bed raked
By the same moon, for the moon will not fill Flesh
like this, will not spill

Upon her skin so much reflected life
And softness. I know should my fingers try The
crotch and spread of these limbs
They would find only marble, blanched

Wood like stone, cool to the core.
But I swear on my lost loves, no whore
Lies like the present moment and desire,
That gray eye so deep within

The body's rooted secrets.

Hard Rain

Sleet fills as it falls
through these February woods.
Subtle as these headstones—
gray, taupe, bone-white—to the eye
are its declensions to the ear.
It lives on analogy.

Grain shifting with a sigh as
the shovel stirs it.
 A winged horde humming.
 Sand spilling down one vast
 hourglass or blown against a
 tin roof in a dust storm.

Choruses beat against
dead leaves
vocatives beyond number,
tinnitus of nylon jacket sleeve,
cheeks raw with listening
to hollow log, iron bark
and upright stone,
or fine distant dust almost
silent into snow.

Rain made durable
enough for winter,
born from the hard facts
in the heat of the sun's
making dream.

Flurry

A dusting merely. From a flint sky a
rubbing of sparks. Rain gone soft
into sentimental white silences.
Batting for the hard-edged houses.

Pointillist homage to the lawns, tight
silver jackets for the gravel beside the
road, one long black satin stain into a
horizon baffled by white dust.

Weightless moths fly unaware through
a world innocent with light, bat my
eyelids and mouth, swarm and change
their minds in the wind.

They will cling or disappear, compact
until they drift us into deafness
or grace, when love finds her voice. Who
can tell from this brief glance.

Snow Tropes

First siftings,
snow in ragged breath
surrounds him.

White spoolings
of flax from machines
bolted to the oily
floors of Massachusetts,

released by spring windows
where young girls, lungs
mesh already,
steal temporary sunshine.

Once in a beard his
breath of snow
fell across his shoulders,
graying ice thin

between the threads,
asthma closing its fist
around his chest.

Feathers off the deck
of the pickup
when we found
the hole in the pillow

and gleefully watched
summer go wrong
with snow,

breathing deeply
until the white
lies were gone.

A Winter's Tale

Hedged twilight. Orange pink
rags over frozen snow.
Cold a thought dead fields think to
hide from thaw and plow.

Stakes of corn lean broken swords
over shallow graves in furrows.
No one remembers. The damp words
wept by April, her theatrical sorrow,

summer open to the flaw and spade.
Nothing but this iron memory,
splints and broken halberds, glory
snapped over winter's knee

warming now by the tavern hearth, melting
the old story down with breath.

Night Driving

My high beams turn the trees to snow,
concrete to linen, fluoresce the gravel and
white lines that flash by like filaments.
From the deep roadside, a pair of eyes
dipped in amber studies the wedge of winter light
with which I freeze the night I pass through,
just ahead of the blackness weighing in behind.

Hard Winter

Soon Mr. Kunstler next door will grab his deck chair
and arthritis and unfold them both into milder air

around the fingerlings of crocus and spokes of willow twisting
in cold fists of wind again today. Mud in pillows

lines the roadside where plows betrayed the edge, chewing
the macadam and shoulder with their wedges

of yellow steel. They bequeathed us cinders in shoals to
rattle our floorboards, fenders, and wheel wells.

Potholes split and spread as if salt were sugar and
roadbeds teeth. Debris clots every sewer.

Lawns meticulously raked through the fall are
littered with branches and limbs, the offal

of a winter for the record books: gray eyelashes of
pine, buggy whips of elm, sycamore, and ash,

whole maple limbs, ten thousand pine cone scraps. A
few low hillocks of snow, dirty bibs wrapped

around each street lamp at the shopping mall remind
us of when plowed Andes of ice were all

we saw for months. Now the promise and mess of change
exhaust us. We resist the call to rearrange,

adapt, plant our green flag in frozen ground, shake
enriched water from plastic jugs around

fence and foundation, rake and stoop, bind
and dispose. Yet light will lift every window blind,

force us to accept again that green ring closing
down our last escape from spring.

Composite Drawings

*are sketches of a possible subject produced from
the experience of an eyewitness*

Encounter

Walking between these narrow lines
gives him exercise and if he pretends
perfectly he will see you

coming toward him between split rail fences,
like those beside the bike path near the lake.
You will not be biking.

You might be walking your dog, a small dog
straining his leash no wider than thread,
his barks so high-pitched and frequent

they seem like sparks above the asphalt.
You assure him the dog is harmless, that it
is saying hello in dog language

and you will both smile as the little dog
sniffs around his shoe and pantleg.
He knows something unexpected about you

but you will not hold it against him.
He will not speak it, not exactly, and you will
have to guess it always as you bring

your hand up, wave, and move on between the
fence posts, admiring the light around their
hand-cut edges, keeping all this

inside a while longer, at home
raking the coals, hearing again
the barks like little bright lights,

feeling the inquisitive nose
against your ankle.

Creation

Stilled inside the music, he allows the
hammers to ride where they will, till
the air and seed it, random
with odd harmonies blown together.

They will feed or lie fallow. He plays,
thumbing the bass, late afternoon
rallying a storm, loosening leaves
and branches asymmetrically to invade

notes just released, jazzing the holly
scraping its brushwork across the sill,
thunder denying closure to bass
and mantel clock, a scale unresolved

but insistent, shivering his house from
the corner of the blackest pane. One
brilliant scar augments the sky, finds
its voice, delivers him.

October Field Corn

Hip to hip
down the ballroom aisles,

taffeta gowns
and sliding shoes,

I am her partner
the wind,

brittle melody
and glance.

I close my eyes
and dance.

Monet's Chickadee

Monet said he wanted to paint
the enveloping air, not the fence posts, tiny
black and white bird, or folds of snow. A
ridiculous idea—without eternity.
Air is thought, Monet said: color, shape,
scratched canvas, what was missed yesterday,
the day before, later this afternoon. Do not leave
without this moment,
everything said to him. You and I are
necessary. How extraordinary.
Together we take possession
of this space. Stand in for them.
Take their names and wait on the light they
need more than life because
light is the air that contains it.
Here, Monet said. Take back
your own stile and fence where a
single chickadee waits forever to
fly away through everything you
breathe in everyday.

Monet settled for this clump of stuff,
insisting beauty can be recognized
because light trembles with feeling,
as if it were afraid to be found out
to be exactly what it is: light, shape, color. The
day is gone when this began,
when this first appeared, when
the creator disappeared.
Yet this air continues to vibrate as if something
mattered because Monet stood out in the cold
before a stile, a fence, a single chickadee,
compelled by air full of snow, and song.

"My Egypt"

After a picture by Charles Demuth, also of Lancaster, PA, 1927, a realist cubist rendering of John W. Eshelman and Sons grain elevators, formerly of 244 N. Queen Street.

And ours here where
we redeem the blank
white face squared
by the sun

flat otherness itself
just down the street
at Eshelman's

where the trucks backed up and
the grain ran
in and out like sand,
sighing when it flowed

famine and feast
we build around
with color and sound

front the sky
with square and pyramid,
house the priest
inside the granary

distant and severe as
any tombstone or
sarcophagus,

the ochre Nile
ferrying the past along
in hieroglyphs,
slaves mortised in memory

stranger
than Akhenaten,
so foreign and close to home

until the human face appears,
eyes for windows, long chin
of plenty,
a brow forbidding, vigilant

the stern father
who hides love in distance
and centuries of dust

bleeding feet
and shoulders under ropes
triangulating death with stone,
God with mathematics

here on our street,
the granary demolished in 1978 to
expand the headquarters

of the Blind Association,
and beneath the black health of
our hills furrowed with corn,
wheat, beans, every grain

under heaven behind this mask, the
imperturbable face
that will not smile

but peals avenues of light
across each feature,
flies from the straining beam in
spear and cylinder.

Breughel's Hunters Return

A bitter cold sky
turquoise as the ice below and
full of wind,
snow and ice everywhere else:
canals, roofs and eaves,
two frozen ponds.

Our focal point, the hunters stand
tall in their left-hand corner
but bend into the wind and the work
of pulling themselves through snow
above their ankles. They have
just reached the precipice above
town. A steep path must wait
unseen a few feet ahead, but we
will never know. A dozen
whippets every size of lean trail
behind like hooks towing the
snow, or plowing it.

Some anonymous small game drapes
its brown fur
over one hunter's shoulder.
How can it be enough?
Their long wooden poles are bare.
From a house front to their left a
sign swings in the wind
from one unbroken hinge,
announcing in smudged Dutch some
unrenderable service.

No face is quite visible.
We are in this together.
Anonymously, they walk ahead, downcast,
weary and cold,
but the fire they walk past

outside the House of the Broken Sign
leaps high in the wind,
endangers the wooden shed
and the hands of the women
tending it with rakes.
What are they burning, and why
waste so much warmth?
Or is the fire already
spiraling into the nearby houses?

Far below, the townsfolk
find themselves diminished by comparison,
but they make up for scale
with numbers. Both ponds are busy with
skaters: some measure how close two
curling kettles come to their goal.
Others brandish hockey sticks like
swords. Three children skate
in matching postures, one young couple
hand in hand. The rest spin and glide all-
black bodies across the flat surface, except
for one small blur
that could be a greatcoat, or
someone in a greatcoat, flat
against the ice, too still in
this frenzy of frozen life.

Three blackbirds sweep the sky
of certainties. All the joy
fanning the hearts and houses of
the skaters and lovers
cannot fly this cold,
three returning hunters with downcast faces,
one chilled pelt pulling at one shoulder
as they walk, ready to descend,
to join the others, poised here forever with
the rest of us proportioned always
somewhere between them.

Model

From my snowdrift blindness
I hear the first graphite scratchings
with wonder, tingle with the slow featherings,
wince beneath the sharp erasures.
I see nothing, but I begin to feel.

The first broad strokes
wash oil into my wounds, and soon my skin
begins to breathe. Cloth presses close to me its
blue stirrings, gold threads of thought.
My eyes open, never to close again. I
will drink in forever these angles,
colors, motions I need not follow,
only absorb.

I never tire of looking at his face,
long and narrow, tipped with a graying beard,
skin worn as the wood around the door.
His eyes are never still. They shoot
their blue-gray gaze everywhere, amazing me.
Those times he steps back suddenly
and smiles, I feel myself glow,
and mirror him.

Each pearl ingrown upon the brown
velvet of my bodice, the exact weight of
my linen collar the color of bone
and heft my body brings against my clothes, the
ringlets by my ears that await
winds that never come: these are
more real to me than she was while
she sat beneath the skylight day
after day. She never held
his attention as I do, and she has gone where
they all go.

I love the silver light that fills
the window when he has gone away.
Its vibrant emptiness calls to me.
I feel its call to shadow and color

palpable as his thumb,
delicate as his three-strand brush
against the tear duct of my eye.
It will find me content, ready and waiting,
moving already toward their hearts.

The Emperor's Clothes: For Sylvia

If only the words were only words,
Chinese stick figures, limping emperors in clothes
embroidered by young girls, legions of them,
only their tiny fingers sly enough
to catch hummingbird and ibis feather, one
robe per day, one only, however
many years in the making, then hidden away.

Extravagantly beautiful, they create deceptions the
eye can cling to, then close with sleep.
So thin, they can live in vast closets and
seem to disappear. They are given spines to hold them up,
yet they too are
disposable, like the girls.

Gown-silk slubs the light each time the
rosewood door swings open—
another one—perhaps alive with blackberries
no larger than a pinpoint, startling red tulips,
waves in which every grain of salt
can be seen, smelled, felt as it rides
into the wound—sliding in beside the others,
exact and elegant, smoothly gliding against
its neighbor, one more perfect body
waiting for its soul.

In the corning dark, the young girls whisper
among themselves the tiny stories they came
to tell and they laugh, as young girls will, at
all that death, at all that
labor nesting shoulder to shoulder, such
narrow lovers hiding their intricate
handiwork, arms motionless by their sides,
reaching only toward the dust
gathering each day below their triple hems.

Spirit Levels

—for Flynn, George, and Seamus

1. Yesterday I found a handwritten poem
   upside down on an endpaper of William
   Carlos Williams' Selected Poems. Just called "Poem," it
   was a playful, bittersweet meditation
   on the distance between careful metrics, syllabics, and
   the fluttering of her skirt in the wind.
   Like everything else about Flynn, the draft was
   very promising.

2. He took his life four years ago
   and I am haunted by his books. A few at a time, they
   are passed along by his father, George,
   a midwife who works with Annie.
   He cannot bear to bag and drop them at
   some local used book sale.
   But since he cannot keep them all, he
   sends some on to me.

   Without exception they are keepers. Mostly
   poetry, *Collecteds* of Rilke, Roethke, as well as the Williams. Heaney's
   Spirit Level was one of our duplicates,
   but Flynn's is filled with thoughtful comments in
   the tiniest, most exact script I've ever seen.
   Except for "Poem," the notes are unique among the books.

3. Perhaps, like me, Flynn heard Heaney
   talking to him in his sleep, cultivating rows
   of articulate turf and glister
   beside the roads, rocks, and megaliths, still
   able to plant around the troubles.
   Perhaps he saw his life recognized at last
   as a worthy sensation that ran along the rims of
   mountains he had always intended to visit, at

least along the rims of deft lines he claimed
instead as his own, another life to live.

4. Now Heaney is gone, too, and I am drawn back
to Flynn's impossibly small notes, troubling all
these surfaces, Heaney's and mine.
I cling to their perfect order, sharp insights and
sharper questions. Yet I hate today
fitting one thing to another, the guff of destiny,
tiny intellections surviving the eye,
the hand, the mind that found them out.

5. Heaney's black and white truths—so far
from black and white—sit securely inside
Flynn's hyper-neat blue addenda.
Come here, they both say, before it
is too late. Save the interlinear
notes one life puts up against another.
Defend against the words setting up
for themselves, denying already the experience forgotten
into the syntax of the next line,
life presumed over and over
in the punctuation of the phrase, the shape
of the consonants, the strict margin of the page.

Cultural Exchange

I read the great poets of catastrophe dumbly.
Slots of the wooden freight cars,
hands and boot-tops, whose last car never passes.

They are machines that refuse to perforate the
sprockets of movie film, or stamp out silver
CDs in iridescent rainbows.

Our trees wave in wind so many frames per
second, our dead digitally alive again in slo-
mo, close enough to feel their breath.

Those old bears cannot rest here. Spray paint
their verses on CARE packages to Third World
book clubs. We have the Folio Society.

Our witnesses can be found on social media.
Their rusty machine-guns are in museums with
the swords and bi-planes and books.

Not bar-coded, they cannot be valued.
On roadside billboards, mass graves would tank. Too
hard to sexualize. And where is the redemption

of suffering by commerce? Our imagination is
a teenage girl asleep in her room, history
the knock on her door. She loves the multiplex.

Their pens would tear up our parking lots,
their Old Testament faces start appearing
on Halloween masks. A fine thing for the children.

Let them mutter off together into the old growth.
We can still catch sight of their campfires winking
in the distance when nothing else is on.

Poetry at Hayfield House

Here between the seasons we have come to
listen. Grackles quarrel
among the oaks, and beveled windows
slide partway open toward the first enticements of
spring. They find our gathered roots
quiet and receptive to freshening sounds.

Here among the halls of anthracite,
the robber baron's castle a classroom now, we
open to blue and green suspicions
with the sons and daughters of the breaker boys who
judged the worth of the baron's black gold, attending
to lines polished like coal

celebrating slag heaps shagged with ice,
sleeves and kerchiefs flecked like old flags
with blood, old dreams gone underground, in
voices that pound like sleet
on the breaker's roof this striking spring day in
Wilkes-Barre, re-opening the vein.

Primary Colors

Green and orange, angled and striped
like a sergeant's sleeve, Binney and Smith
Crayola crayons in the big box came

stepped in risers, graduated organ pipes
of color, notes to play over pages of fat
black lines, dull as geometry.

You could press color like a valve,
darken it with muscle,
enlighten it with grace. Overlap blue

on yellow, green on orange,
and find yourself creation's very nub.
Emptiness was doomed.

Wrapped paper peeled in neat curls
like planed wood. You rebuilt the afternoon. A
rainbow of names colored the sky:

cerulean and Prussian blue,
magenta, aquamarine, turquoise.
Each word a new breath against your tongue.

You made the black lines home
for too long, incandescing from within,
smoothing to an oil-paint gloss, blending

shades into single new colors with tissue
paper rubbed against the hunter's cheek and
the log home of the lonely squirrel.

At last you left the lines behind.
Planned, penciled in, erased,
surprised the sunburst guitar fading

from midnight to noon by perfect
invisible steps, speckle-flake
fenders on a hot-rod coupe, the secret

white square reflected by a water bubble, its
prismatic rainbow edge. A dabbler brushed
by love, at last you took

illusion for a slow ride, found in your own line
and shiftiness better play than inerrancy,
and felt each shade of difference glow.

Urban Muse

Walking among the cursive letters,
the light rasp of the nib
follows the electric ebb and flow,
the recurrent suspicion
that among the neat houses of words
lives the number he seeks.

Down symmetrical alleys and streets
darkness throws the streetlight switch,
the clear grid of bus route
and subway he already missed between six
o'clock's alarm and the kiss
he dreamt of waking her with.

Film Noir

Bourbon unsteadies the glass, dies
In the mirror by the bed. I close her eyes.
The streets are wet again, the street light In
halos down the aisles of the night.
One neon strand pulses like a nerve
Across the street, a curved
Scar reflected in the dirty glass.
Her face hangs in the air like smoke From
her cigarette. Then the rain spoke With
bored fingers on the roof: Listen. You
expected different? From a woman Who
rocks herself to sleep each night With
dreams like yours, violent and slight, Two
grainy reels in black and white?
Even the moon forgets you tonight.

Packet

The tin roof records the rain
All afternoon, slow syllables again And
again, schoolboy summer by rote
In a rocker on the porch. What he wrote Lies
in an attic among old wicker and gilt In a
wood-slat trunk, brass and dowel-built An
age ago, filed away when the sun Corrected
proof by one window and June No longer
hung in the air with light
Strokes and wise, a tale accurate and slight
Caught just before the wind sailed,
The packet steamed north, and the words failed.

One on One

I can't remember
why I left it in the yard,
the cheap rubber basketball
my son spurned.
Perhaps in the vain hope
the collie might push it up
and down.

Nor do I remember
when it went strange,
bleached whiter than paper.
I do remember booting it
away as I mowed down summer,
sending it corner to corner.

Soon I never had to bother.

It slept out of my way
behind pines or hedgerow,
wedged by the fieldstone wall
crumbling in the wide yard's
lower half.

Then it left
the regular round paths.

Rose up into the dogwood,
a communion wafer
among the pink and white tongues.

Sat in the empty doorway
framed by the roofless shed
with intolerable longing.

Wedged in a vacant pane
jauntily, making the other
eyeless window wink.

One April dawn it lay
at the apex of a triangle
formed by three storm-blown twigs.

Once it deflated just enough
to ride the round corner post
of a neighbor's chain-link fence.
I scanned it with horror through
my birding binoculars
like Marlow stumbling on Kurtz's
severed heads.

Each time I see it
the place where I stand
is changed.

And that blind eye
looks everywhere.

Today it appeared
for the first time
outside the fence,
skirts muddy from the rain.
Quiet by the driveway,
it sits just across from my window.

I dread the slow
rising of that other moon
through the empty trees
tonight.

Figure Skating

Come in upon the skates of light
alone. Turn quickly.
They will not see you spinning, only
hear the slur of ice.

Let your hands rope slowly
above your head,
then let them slowly
fall. They will never

believe you have not
stopped turning.
They turned with you.
They turned you.

When you stop,
stabbing down the muscle
they forgot, they
will never forgive you.

Melanoma

A word so beautiful cannot
harm me, she said smiling,
her eyes, wrists, ankles
reneging already the lease
of skin.

Last night the word fell
so ripely, lip and tongue, I
whispered it for hours.

An Italian river olive green,
slow and heavy as oil, olive
trees along the shore
beside pitted columns, fluted
and roofless, small relics
of a smaller deity.

Greek liquor the color of rust,
fire alive in a liquid base
that turns men into beasts
and women into butterflies.

A girl in pigtails who plays
on the sand in absolute sunshine, a
straw hat shielding her face from all
she will never know,
or guess at. Nurse cuts
her bread, Camembert, and pears.

The refrain my Renaissance lover
sings beneath my window,
my other name, echoes of his lute
among the plucked orchids
lining my marble windowsill.

A beautiful word cannot lie,
she said softly to the air.
That is its reward for a life
given over to suffering.

Vases

These days possess no shape,
only duration.
They should be so many vases
holding in their hollow palms some
vivid portion,
worthy to retain
by size and curve exact the
matter in between.

A bud vase
for pinched winter days
when even one narrow thought
must be bought somewhere else
and carried home in a box,
but preserved with thanks.

A squat crock
thrown from tough, braided clay still
mud-brown with earth,
a maw like a cave
with room enough to save
three fields of wildflowers.

Even an old jelly jar,
juice glass of the poor–
rare now, almost gone,
that when I was a boy
more than once held a dandelion
too lovely to throw away.

The Calling

I missed today just this physical fact.
This enticement. This act.
The lift of the pen barrel against
The index finger pad
Compressing nerves and fingerprints.
The precise lift and angle—
30° between nail and knuckle—
Of the braced pen where it slants
Against the middle finger.
The considering balance of the thumb
And slight scratching hum
Of point upon paper.
I am not called by meaning but desire.

Song

Leaf-printed sunlight on the floor,
swaying. Cutout shadows playing
against the things themselves, green

to the bone and greener in this noon window
frame. Holly thorns of blood. Mimosa grace.
Open palms of sycamore.

All blur and slur across the carpet.
Reflect, they say. Give back again in
black and white and gray. Ripen

each berry with shadows of decay.
House the sun and rain. Walk in and
out of them, singing the little all we
can, and the all we cannot say.

Alternative Light Sources

*provide visible and invisible light at various intervals to
help investigators locate and visually enhance evidence*

In Crete

I saw god,
The slab of his shoulders
Where the world sits, his haunch
Where spears break
Above hoof-blades, a head
Wide for wisdom and eyes To
penetrate worlds unborn,
Horns to hold our differences
In one sustaining thought,
Uproot our lies and tear the sky
With storms of sympathy
For men and women lost In
their frail skin,
Bereft of everything
But the sound of hoof beats ringing.

Easter Island

Inexplicable stone faces
angle toward the shore,
its tufts of weeds, black basalt
slag of the eternal sea.

Rites hide forever behind
steep foreheads, family
resemblances
of woe and insight.

Dragged across pea-coal turf by
carts, by hundreds, by a faith
moving mountains
but carving them first.

Gone. Wind and guano and silence.
We stand beneath their long brows
and noses. They wish for hands and
shoulders to shrug.

We wish for stone hearts
below the surface of the ground
on a level with the sea.

Blessing Way

The shaman, a hummingbird cupped gently in
his hands, blesses the boy with words:

Live your life lightly, no better or worse
as you criss-cross the earth than a skipped stone,
badger, white-tailed deer, or hummingbird
no bigger than the blink of a second yet
who flies in beauty everywhere.

For us humans, however, our task
is to chant the world, to learn the songs of
blessing. You must speak
to the holy people every day.
Chant to them. They are everywhere.

The holy people make the air nervous.
Sand painting is our door between
the worlds of the holy people
and the ordinary people
so that beauty may be maintained.

You must chant like this and listen
to your own words. They must be your words: Unless
I think, there is no word.
Unless I look, there is no world. Unless
I move, there is no life.

So the sky becomes my sky,
so the lake becomes my lake
and the earth becomes my earth.
The woman I love knows who I am.
And in these things I will live on.

Then he released the hummingbird to
fly in beauty everywhere.

Piercings

In Malaysia, the two days of Haikusam
celebrate Lord Muruhan's victory by spear over evil.
Flesh becomes the pierced world and the god enters
backs, tongues, cheeks. Prayer and water prepare.
Frenzy grips the faithful as the first dart bloodlessly
skewers his mouth. The carnival rides turn and spin
around him. This festival is Hindu.
The Tunnel of Love, Roundabout, Merry-Go-Round with
its thousand lights. Tethered by a hundred hooks,
another man pulls a float through the food stands.
At the monkey god's appearance, the mutilations
increase and carry the god closer. "Bel! Bel!" shout
the encouraging thousands, meaning
the sacred spear. Rapture banishes pain,
suppressing the blood, holding it inside
to vibrate to the god's voice like the bumping cars
and bubbling lard, the barking dogs, and the nods of the
entranced leading the thousands as one, tawdry
and profound, into the sacred cave,
up the 274 steps to where the carved altar
plunges its fishhook deep beneath the mountain side.
The world is flesh. It must be entered and held.

The Shaman's Apprentice

First the giant ants,
then the fire ants,
then the tree ants,
his tongue spread against the bark like
one wing for the long flight back
because the healing songs
will swell the tongue, too, to
slow the routine words into
beauty and wisdom

Over and over the shaman's breath
interrupts his own, pushing down his
throat the wiser air

Into the depths for days
without food, slapping
the pests that sting the spirit
where it sits to pull
energy from the trees
and beasts, the red
hives humming,
brimming with fire,
while overhead god's
thousand eyes wink and
reappear

New breath swells his chest
and air becomes a savoring to
share

Endless practice
of the song of the widowed heart,
songs of the hernia
and shrunken testicle,
dead child mutilated by dogs,

crops who disobey
the sun, fused twins,
pigs loose among the low hills,
the song of the singer of song

sweeping mouth and lungs
with sacred smoke, words arising of
themselves in mist

to cloud the wounded,
wash fear down
the valleys of their bodies as
rain, rinse their ears
with their own naming songs,
melodies in fingerprints, words
become their flesh by the
stingings of his spirit,
priesthood of his suffering and
his song.

Sunday Afternoon, Kinzer, PA

Perfect Sunday afternoons in mid-July Amish
families, too, rest and move
along the narrow roads, their severe garb
clean and pressed, black serge trousers and
aprons, lilac and royal blue and violet shirts
and dresses, filmy over-smocks
and bonnets on the young women, glowing
as the square gray single-horse buggies
clatter slowly by, the horse's hoofs
catching the sunshine in sparks, harness gleaming, gray
canvas rolled up in the rear
like an old porch awning.

They stay on the safe connecting roads—
Dry Tavern, Osceola Mill, West Pequea Cave, Pumping
Station or Smoothing Iron—
as the tourists fly over the numbered highways.
Children in their straw hats and bright white shirts
smile shyly and wave as I pass,
their elders in metal bifocals like so many
scholars of medieval philosophy,
straw-caked plums of horse dung everywhere
they go—dust to dust to dust—and nothing
sentimental, thank you, in the callused hands and
shrewd dealing, the farms rich as Midas,
entrepreneurial carpentry, hand-crafts, repairs.

Iron backbone and the coulter of faith.
In but not of. Plain fare and work till Sunday.
Watch the contrails dwindle back to clouds as
they wait to cross Rts. 340 or 772,
as unhurried as the multi-colored plates
are driven, the hum of their straining engines a
temporary whine soon replaced by

corn soughing in the wind, the creaking
windmill by the barn, lowing milk cows
and the barking hound who trips another
rat beneath the milk house.

Promises

*"All holy desires grow by delay. If they diminish
when delayed, they were never holy desires."*
—St. Gregory

Turn, counter-turn, hide to seek, then satisfy
one briefest instant, deepest light and warmth to
the center of what is, or one-tenth
of its ten-thousandth. And why
makes do with slopes of snow that will not last past
April. He, too, is seasonal,
death rebirth death, summer autumnal in
her delicate bones and profligate past. Tap
lightly the door set into the rock.
The voice is hollow and the night is here.
A flame winds down from the perimeter
of low hills. It will arrive with the zero dark.
    Descend, turn, look up. The tiny lantern-case swings
    toward you, grows beneath the hidden face.

Chalice and Madonna

This ancient chalice
knobby with jewels
hefts like a broadsword or a jousting lance.
What muscular priests it took to lift so
much Eucharist.
Upholding its heavy ecstasies
must have shivered sinew
up a thousand sleeves and
exhausted doubt with pain.
In that strict romance
each player strove to lift
from his bowl of clay a soul,
hoist it by main strength of will
with arms massed and taut
as this precious metal skin.
Silver spools, a foam of golden surf
lap the inlaid surface of that world
between continents of ruby, emerald, and amethyst: A
universal map, rigid and serene.
A plan beyond price
where no pore of space
escaped significance.

With what struck hearts
those clustered monks
must have gazed as you rose above them like
another sun,
casting out spears of light beneath
the dusky sanctuary lamp.
Sweating in their coarse copes as
drafts in cattails curled and froze
around their naked feet,
they must have hurled their hearts like coals
into the ice they knew too well:
wooden spoons and bowls,
whips and nettle-cloth, a silence

heavy as the weight of stars—all
melted into blood
and mingled in your shallow bowl.
Backs bent from bowing to the hoe
straightened in the rough-cut pews.
Knotted bellies eased in
the bliss you released and
poured into moments
strung like beads and hung across eternity,
moments set like jewels in a brutal age
poised between rage and sleep
when each icy corridor
of cloistered stone
echoed with the choirs of belief.

In your service the manly rows ignore
the perfect body painted on their wall,
cannot admit or trace
even with one fingertip the
young Renaissance heart
beating beneath a breast
like a bowl filled with snow,
a heart the Madonna strives
herself to still
with the silk shawl
she pulls so tight
between such delicate fingernails.

In the Name of the Rose

I cannot see him anymore. I trusted the
mirror I myself nailed to the tree,
believed in the other middle ages, frost
identical with fog, the sublime choked

in its crib, its wool cloak stiff with blood, dogs
into wolves, and the raped child.
I am here among half-truths, daily violations,
oxen-eyed corpses

twisted beside the hillside crosses, the
drowned monk in the vat of wine
body and blood, gently stirring sacrifice.
I am alone in the scriptorium

in the middle of the night, thick
shut books, each chain a rope of moonlight.
All we know is on the skin of sheep, famous
for their ignorance. In this half-light

their pages squeak like slit lambs.
I light one candle, illuminate one swarm of
images. I light one candle and stare into
the future. I cannot get warm.

Frankincense

In nearly every known culture
frankincense has been sacred,
its acrid pleasures ratifying the ladder leading
to the soul. Spirit itself,
the godhead, approachable through scent.

Battling the charred grease of sacrifice,
putrefaction of the body, they declared the
unseen truer because unseen.
They ate deep breaths and prayed, slight
sawing sounds of breath for truth.

Obsessive sense the door of mystery
opening on the world beyond knowing.
Remarkable and sad, experience
doomed by its own perfection, absolute
beyond forgetting.

I yearned for the frankincense
I could not become, wrapped myself in tape
soaked and sacramental. I too would die to
be born, be carried through air
and loved as a pleasure beyond words.

Grind the bone, I prayed,
to powder. Cover your face with me.
Inhale. I am still yours. Molecule to
molecule, matter straight to mind. We
are perfect. We are one.

Inheritance

How familiar he is, the eldest son.
The slog, fret, endless measly sacrifice
dawn to dusk, all marked by the same absence of
mystic release, illumination.

Sizzling grease of lamb vaporizes the air
already drunk with music and wild song.
There he stands, still filthy under his long purple
cloak, twinkling with gold rings to spare.

I have no rings, cloak, or grass-fatted goat, not
even a rowdy late-night shebang
to savor and regret. I feel the pangs
he deserves. Death and rebirth I cannot.

All I hear as I tend the clogged sewers is
his plea: My son, all I have is yours.

Money

No wonder we love Old Parley. He
stands in for everything.
Folding his dirty self away we
only need to count to sing

the world into our pocket.
Gold rings, slick kisses, granite
monuments. Money is the socket light
takes for granted

and held up to the light, money glows.
Its halo assures
artist and priest plenty of
recovery room.

It makes the future
visible in its crystal ball.
Look. The needed suture is
sewn, the unneeded gall

stone rolls from the tomb.
We are still here, paying.
Money is the womb
of happiness, moistly weighing

alternatives to grief. Keep
it coming! she cries and
soon the little thief
bounces at her breast.

The Offices of Lust

She travels their dreams on
feet lost in flowers,
tiny feet (they are certain) white as milk, wet
with dew, yet warm.
They hear the soft crush of tiptoes
along the carpeted silence
as their eyes close.

The wind shivers her skirt
where she passes their windows all day, lifts
her hair to reveal
one seashell ear, impossibly small, one
slender hoop of gold in suspense.
Heels upon the sidewalk send remorse code,
whispers of nylon into punctuated hearts until
their knuckles whiten
around their plastic pens.

In the huddled traffic nosing home
she appears in a driver's window frame,
a red metal toll booth, lacquered like her lips,
drumming the wheel with lacquered fingertips,
eyes upon the stopped surge ahead.
Each time she shifts upon her leather seat, the
voice on their radios goes dead.

At home, wives bend above their meals
until they are consumed, dreaming other lives
with other mysteries of men,
wielding the past like steak knives,
horrible and sharp. He hears it scrape the bone.

The Wages

She has rare skill with skin,
all the cultures of the flesh.
Maps all the sites of sin, their
archeology of ash.

Coiled upon the chaise,
her body a cocked gun,
you will pray to squeeze
her trigger of oblivion.

She will try your piety
before the bar of lust,
in her *auto-da-fe*
convert one heretic to dust.

On the heart's harp she plays
in time, but prefers to sing the
chest the heart displays.
Follow her dowsing tongue.

On the seventh day she rests
her head upon your thigh,
names one by one her beasts
and winks her needle's eye.

Between her knees,
you swim back the way you came.
She banishes your fears,
then banishes your name.

She sends flesh and blood to
sea, alone upon the ark. On
the dismal coming flood, they
sail into the dark.

She will resurrect you
on the third day, fourth
and fifth, unscrew
the stone and push you forth

risen from the dead,
speaking through tongues of
flame around your head
and singing *The Song of Songs*.

She witnesses your fever
as you rise into the clouds, the bliss of
your second coming. Forever comes
and goes, briefer than a kiss.

Remorse

No butcher would own
this slaughtering of self:
brute hacking strokes

that mutilate instead
of severing,
advertise the mess

yet leave the carcass
quivering, white bone aslant
where the skin gapes

like a stage curtain. All
his sharp practices
come down to this:

One corpse of days
as if gristle were the end, not
dead weight to be axed.

Lay it on the paper waxed
for the purpose
and throw it on the scale.

Let the butcher's nail
judge the cut
and fix the cost.

In Praise of the Soul

Practicing eternity is hard
here, sublime with clutter
and trash. One pound of lard is
enough to flutter

St. Benedict from prayer:
this useful mass,
rites of the renderer,
slick soul Bossy's body left.

She can derail a saint's
memento mori skull
staring from his desk. Paint
bone blue, stick a pencil

in his ears, rake a patch
pirate-like over one eye:
however small the batch,
that white fat won't fly.

Thank God again for heat
and an iron fry pan,
hunger's regular retreat from
greasy contemplation

into French toast or eggs.
What came too near once
can still satisfy and plump
belief, ounce by ounce.

Leafmeal, or Herb-of-Grace

From her high window
she mingles the autumn leaves, elm
pin oak maple ash,
dry dancers through the trees.

Today she hates her heart, its
dry circle of desires,
the way it constricts her throat. It
does nothing well but hurt,

she thinks, sipping rue as
the wind throws color in
galaxies past her eye:
No one really cares

that we drift alone
beneath old hedge or stone, until
someone we loved stops by to
find us powder already,

deserting hedge or stone
in all our fine particularities,
to atone before the snows.
So much dust upon a bone.

Children's Night Prayer

From the old mother
    of the everyday
        deliver us
    mealworm and katydid
        spotted frog and moth

You are too beautiful
    for us all together
        and apart
    we cannot return to you
        likeness and soul

We sit on the back steps
    watching the sun leave
        quietly as the gray cat
    next door into the shadows
        of the lilac stems

We do not know her name
    anymore, she is invisible
        we only hear her paws
    go lightly through dead leaves
        where the sun cannot find her

Only the crickets look
    alive, seen by our
        closed eyes held
    the way our hands
        hide our knees

We are alone again
    together, cold entering
        our canvas shoes we
    dream ourselves awake
        in case sleep never comes

Analytical Drift

is the variability in a method, test, or procedure where results gradually deviate from the norm or expected range

Awakenings

I unlimber my dreams to find a TV Gesturing
soundlessly from the corner.
The tiny people grow more desperately silent,
But I am dumb with them, and deaf.
My outstretched hand dwarfs them,
Then slides away across the glass
In tracks of dust. Their flat bodies walk, Run,
embrace, and their flat lips
Flutter like moths. Closing my eyes, I
bow my head until I almost hear
The faint hum our lives make together.

In Praise of Reading

—for Jene and Jetta

I imagine all
I have read (so many winters)
not quite lost as I feel
with mind's empty fingers

finding each cell shapelier
in its sack of tears,
each blood drop riper
in its rounding house

because thought's weight
will ballast the machine
of forgetfulness, once taught
inform both muscle and vein

Dialectic

What to hold against the great silence but
noise refined. Patois whispered moonlit
under breadfruit leaves.
Lines articulate with moonlight to talk
night across the sea.

Rumors of far islands into pidgin
run through narrow, steaming towns.
Our shadows pull us slowly across
the moonlit beach. Water
cools us. We push off. We do not speak.

Digital

I loved habit first to still the shaking,
made ritual my daily crawl,
loved machines—so blunt, so factual,

carrying breath, heartbeat, pulse, marching
me toward the kitchen, or else on eternal
slippers to the sky.

Green readouts of a greener time—
clock, fridge, coffee pot, stove. Less is more
again and I am tired, with stairs to climb.

Rusty seconds need oil, fraying veins
electrical tape. I must sleep. It rains.
I dream in ones and zeros of zeros and ones.

You Could Look (It) Up

The five o'clock sky lours
over the shopping center. Over Ross:
Dress for Less. Famous Footwear. Marshall's.
The yellow brick and poured concrete surround
the bright flourishes of their names.

I think the word I want is "lours."
Though it is getting toward evening, the sky seems
too dark for the hour. It hangs
upon the flat roof-edge of the shopping center as
if it could drip down over the facades.

At the same time, the dark sky seems
as if it could extend forever: steep,
unsegmented, conscious.
Because the word seems intentional,
rounder than "moon" in my mouth.

I do not know exactly what "lour" means
or if the sky above the shopping center did it when
I started writing, for the sky has changed,
grayed in perfect harmony with what I already knew
before I stopped in here, alone, for a bite of supper.

Apple

Nearer than any shadow, the other life
follows, ripens in every gesture,
each crow's foot branching like a glory
narrow furrows on narrow faces.
It beetles close. Inhabits. It breathes
in each exchange oxygen for something else.
It will not rent the tree house
to anyone but you. More intimate
than any answer to any question,
the other life defines gravity by falling.

It consumes the observable apple from
its first cracking open into taste to the
slight stickiness of its beads down the
fine pale hairs of her chin,
each glint sunlight stakes on the ruddy skin,
mottled with beauty as an autumn leaf.
It holds all in abeyance as it waits on:
Disappearance held in the hand, puckered
star to stem, one pale serrated crater
browning, its weight gone
from the palm, empty as the eye's mirror,
empty as the fruit tree of winter.

At Bay

Mere things sit silently, at bay.
    Yet resist with dull, inanimate will. The
    piano preens its mahogany gloss
Behind a wide and vacant smile. In
    the corner one glass eye
    Scans our empty hours a while
Longer. Three oblique angles
    Where the ceiling joins two walls Fill
    the mirror. No spider redeems
The scene, as no breeze collects
The curtain folds, as heavy
    With airless being as lungs collapsed
    Before windows like blank stares.

Calibration

I will weigh the consequences at
the depot on railroad scales, an
auditorium for whales,

or on the hospital step-up crib with
iron quoits where the obese
search for a new rib.

Perhaps by microgram
and the blind justice
of the atom

where it moves invisible,
one fell germ
into one cell wall.

Precincts

Weakness will not do.
Not lapses or frailty.
Sin is too conscious,
Too ripe with ease
And the sliding moon.
Pessimism grinds hours
To dust among the crickets,
And failure is safe as fact. But
when no turning back Teases,
and lungs pulled taut Collapse
instead, the air
Lost but not the thought
Of air, its cinnamon taste Still
ripening the lips,
Then, one step beyond the floor,
You may drop into the rare
Precincts of exact despair.

Syllogism

You will feel the resemblance
When reminded of the sea
Pulling away where you stood
Rooted near the edge, sand
Eroding instep, heel, and toe
Until you tilt in place,
Raked clean by what you loved.

You will recognize at once The
vacuum of grief, the tide When
you lie down alone,
Heavier than wet sand on skin,
Ice drifting from the poles Toward
the body of the sun
Going down in waves, and come close.

You will understand exactly
When the wind picks its way inland
Across the bones of the corn,
The closed pores where the moon freezes In
white pools, the abandoned trees
Gesticulating in silence because
They no longer believe in the sea.

Race

Readiness. More. Readiest. On the mark
Poised. Heaved up muscle and nerve, the tight curl
Ligament snakes around the bone. The swirl Adrenaline
sprays along the vein's dark
Lanes. Blood boiling into the tensed heart.
Fingertips in cinders, balls of the feet
Pressing pain against the blocks. What defeat
Thrusting hope conceives before the start.

Now. Now. Uncoiling energy hurled Far
beyond this gunshot, his body dead
Weight to thought, one moment of pure speed
Flying past the rapt faces of the world
This once, pounding heart and footfall, blind trust
Until the end, one thread above the dust.

Momentary

Leaving duty flood-lit on my desk
I prowl rooms narrowing with dusk, snap
on the table lamps and gas fire where
the dog promptly parks, require Bach's
energy asleep in the black speakers
dreaming the death of fact. They hold
him lovingly back.

Old comforts will not quiet his hunger, nor
my usual addictions. I was younger before
these circling lights and violins
caught the ceramic wood that never burns,
only chars like the sooty clouds outside.
My heart in its wide case weighs the tide. The
dog looks up to ask, "Is it time?"

Tears

Be careful with them.
They fall down for years,
dry up but only seem
spent. Clouds reappear.

Fall for their tricks,
salt defines the rain
forever: oceanic,
one titanic water stain.

Surprise them with joy.
They will repay you with
tears. Grow
because, in spite of them. How?

Smile on, refuse
their queue. A Cheshire cat's
got nothing more to lose. (Well,
yes, there's that.)

Nostalgia

Innocent print clogged highways and cornrows, winding
two-lanes of sentiment and news

county line to seat in a red Oldsmobile turning
92,000 Sunday. We'll never feel

again the letters sweep a light blue page,
billboard capitals on clear margins, an age

before dinner when the burgundy leather cools
in the night air, draws us together

in prosaic affection, all our assertions fixed to
paper until the years and letters mix

humming tires, low ballads on the radio, plain
words flashing past the open windows

a blur like the trees, absolutely true.

Equanimity

Today I will let the squirrels claw their way into
the bird feeders and tulip bins,
the vents and all along the ceiling beams,
shred my insulation and scratch in peace for
whatever fiberglass or plaster grail fulfills a
squirrel's deepest dreams.

Let that rat or hydrocephalic mouse
alone to patrol the kitchen after dark
on his tiny tap shoes and raid the dog's dish at
his leisure, as he did two nights ago, leaving a
trail of cryptic spaghetti
in hieroglyphs across the vinyl floor.

Ignore the spiders in the bathroom
who hang their Belgian doilies out to dry
in both corner-windows, above my wife's line
of mournful pantyhose, dwarfed and wrinkled
as a race of pygmies crucified
and dried to husks. Ignore the cockroach, too,

who salutes me from the drain before I shave,
his antennae intercepting news of rain.
The rabbits may have their ration of petunias and
the sparrows Pollock my Volkswagen's roof. The
dog may claim our waste cans for her own.
Just this once I'll let the fall persuade itself

to winter without arguments from me.
Let the trees slide every sodden leaf
straight down my roof until the gutters groan.
After the flood I'll sit upon the basement stairs
sailing arks made from folded shells
of monthly bills and filled with all my sins.

Opticals

Lens after lens fitted to my face,
The iron tree massive and immovable But
the lenses finely ground, innumerable And
subtle their interplay of spaces,
Like tongue and word, loving contradictions
Refining life in light upon the wall.
Narrow the means of change, unspeakable Its
visions. Then the slow course of fictions, The
trance of negatives in the darkened office And
chance of time, the invisible voice
Gently prodding through choices soon so close That
yes and no become a new consensus.
Until through all the blurring years I wear
The knowledge so near, I hardly know it's there.

Optimism

After a certain interval of living,
one can begin to fear
that he remains alive primarily
to experience sentences like this:

"British regulators decided to delay the
creation of human-cow hybrids
for about a year or two because of concerns that
mixing the two species
could be controversial." *

And yet come to believe
that despite its vast continents of
loss, all its wicked slippages, life
is good.

* "Findings," *Harper's* (March 2007), 96.

Close Surveillance: Expert Witness

Zeno's Progress

Grandma on the way to the mailbox,
her tiny forward-leaning steps
full of Parkinson's and the brittleness
of 86, in white cotton-terry stretch slippers
with paper-thin soles because the callus
blooms above her arthritic heel
until every other week she limps
to the podiatrist, as she does today with her impossibly
small shuffling steps
through the bright first debris of spring
around the leftover winter pine cones,
branches, pebble grains, humps
in the macadam, especially the small
volcanoes where the ferns push their way each
May right through the driveway surface, their
feathery unfurlings so at odds
with a rootedness able to push
millimeter by millimeter against what
must seem to a plant's brain seamless granite
but who will push anyway because
what else can you do, programmed to move,
intercept the air with seed, open
your little umbrella as far as it will go,
push on until resistance ceases
as if by some magic incantation you spoke
without knowing it, merely being
what you are, until you find yourself among
the light at last, and who you are takes a
shape you could hardly dream of
below ground, the size of the steps no matter, the
mass of the seed unimportant,
like the diminishment the world insists on
around the tiny space you occupy
that shrinks by halves as you move, struggle
through a blackness that seems invincible,
the pointlessness of the effort the whole

point because you cannot read the code and
enact it at the same time because the goal
disappears more quickly
the closer you get, and yet there will be an end,
space will yawn open, just when your strength gives
out it will all change, and you will discover

the light hidden all along in the script
handed down into the invisible places, the
care with which your life refused itself
darkness, the strength you hoarded so long to
get to just this point where you could refuse to
stop or fail one more morning,
the letter of the law still closed away
but the spirit coming nearer
with each barely visible step,
green and greener.

First Things

Grandma takes on
    the obit page,
        fingers bent

around the edge of
    one more day.
        She chides

the letting go,
    the surrender of friends, lays
        down

the re-creased paper,
    wipes her hands
        on her starched apron,

struggles to her feet
    and thrusts her walker
        straight at the

    whistling kettle.

Ascent

Grandma drifts noiselessly away in
the ancient hot air balloon
she found on a postcard yesterday: bright
copper guy wires, white Victorian Easter
basket, colored sheeting
hand-stitched in quilted rows
around a plaque painted
with her name, all of it rippling
around the superheated air.

It has been a long time
already since the squares of land far
below held a neighbor's name,
spires or bells a promise.
But the air is pure,
sun and moon next door.

Her hands upon the basket rails
shake with every tremor,
but she has grown light
in the lighter air: shallow breathing, tiny
meals, fitful sleep.

When the anchor rope first fell away she
feared the loss of everything below, only
to find it takes this long
to gather lift enough to catch
the graceful curve of earth, and room enough
to let it go.

Joss Stick

Unlike the chickadees she loves, Grandma
moves across the ground like the mourning doves:
delicately off-center, asway
in mid-motion forward. A chickadee's
appearance, though, weight, and aptitude for
fun. Quickness haunts the memories her
body builds on every day, clouds
the Parkinson's with echoes of grace.

"Look! A joss stick. That's what it's called. Smell! It's
Chinese incense. Down at the Dollar Store."

Two calligraphic birds learn the golden chore
above a monk's swaybacked temple floor.
They fly without moving their paper wings
or leaving their paper sky. They begin to sing.

Out Like a Lion

Onion grass and crocus
baffle the air above today's sleet and snows.

Grandma plugs in the mixer when
she meant the can opener,

stares sullenly from the baked bean can to
the mixer and back again.

I replace the mixer with the opener. Her
eyes spring up, and glare.

They melt first, then freeze.

Murdering Grandma

I would like to sucker punch Grandma
when she dodders in front of me down the hall or
forgets where she put her pill box
in plain sight on the kitchen table.

I could pull out her withered fingernails
one at a time with the corn-on-the-cob tongs
when she talks baby-talk to the dog—
"I believe that dog thinks he can talk!" which
is now on its fifth dog—
or when she uncorks another inanity
repeated thrice weekly for twenty years.
"You just never know what's coming!" "Put
it all in God's hands, Bernice."

Well, hell, Jesus had hands
but they couldn't hang on very long.

I could put her out in the yard
a couple nights a week so the rest of us could
get a good night's sleep for a change without
her creeping like a big mouse around the
house all night from bed
to chair to day-bed to sofa. Tell me
other old people with even more ailments than
she has wouldn't die for an apartment like
hers on the third floor. But oh, no,
just because she's lived here 22 years
she thinks she has the run of the place. I
don't know how much more I can take
from those thyroid pop-eyes or that bent
little shuffle that never gets anywhere.

It will almost certainly happen
when once more she tries to help and save,
like cutting the grains from a two-inch cob of

leftover corn, showering half of them over the
kitchen floor she can no longer
bend to clean or pick up. The exact moment
might well be when, whisk broom
and sopping rag in hand, I rise
from my knees to get back to the dishes steaming in
the sink to be handed a knife—

serrated edge, a tiny Solingen scimitar with
a point like a needle—and hear, "That's a
sharp knife. Be careful."

"She's a saint," they all say.
May be. She's innocent as a potato,
I'll grant you that, and as thick-skinned.
I will ride gleefully down the coal-chute
to hell as soon as I've done it, still hearing
the crabbed echo of that spindly voice
scraping eternity away like knuckles
of hard cheese, "I told that poor boy time
and again. He just wouldn't listen."

• • •

Having just killed Grandma in a poem, it
was with momentary surprise
I saw her totter past me
sitting deep in thought upon the couch.

I'm not sure she saw me. I am only
300 lbs. or so, on a good day, and her radar
often makes me feel small.
Then again, I thought, perhaps her ghost

forgot what came next, too, and is condemned to
circle our small downstairs searching
herself out among the upholstered befuddlement of
twenty years ago, chasing down

her doppelganger until God takes pity and butterfly nets her mid-shuffle.

"Oh," she says, turning toward me as she labors on, "I thought you were the dog."

Scouts

We are all dying
and refusing to die.

Leaning with Grandma
into the wind

that never stops.
She falls toward

a future that loves her madly
and will not let her go.

She tramps in
from the kitchen, inside

shoes growing larger
each week.

She hunts me down.
"I am," she says, and stops.

Each house needs
a scout

to forget the trail,
mirror the inside

of the window
with the see-through self

we thought we knew.
I stand beside her

looking beyond the snow
falling through both of us.

Grandma Meets Anubis

One day in summer
Grandma leans over the chrome railing of the bed.

> *Let's pretend we're Egyptians and figure out*
> *What I should take along for the journey*

You'll need your sweatshirts: "Tweety Bird:
Little Bird, Big Attitude", and "I'm retired.
This *is* what I do." Then there's "Don't forget
my Senior Citizen discount!" and "National Register of
Historic Persons." Do you want the Irish cape
and tam-o'-shanter we brought from the Avoca Woolen Mills?

> *Right. And just a little sentimental jewelry*
> *like Uncle Ed Staab's ruby ring*
> *and Mother's single pearl necklace. Of course, some*
> *representative refrigerator art*
> *from kids and grandkids. Your two books.*

Tussy deodorant. You're their only customer.

> *Very funny. I don't sweat anymore*
> *anyhow. All dried up.*

Plastic bags and twist-ties, of course,
30-gallon green yard bags to the little clear
freezer bags. We can use them, with some judicious
folds of Saran Wrap, for the internal organs,
then stack them neatly in plastic wash baskets.

> *True. Neatness is next to Godliness. You*
> *can't be too careful with leftovers.*

A couple electric heaters, lots of march
music. Bill's WW II decorations.

> *He was good for something once, wasn't he? He*
> *even saved lives before ruining others.*
> *Maybe it evens out.*

A gross of dust cloths. Let's face it, dust to dust . . . A
cell phone. You'd never last a day—
an hour—twenty minutes—without that.

> *Your time is coming, Mister. Listen for the ringing.*

Another gross of Bounce fabric softener
sheets. A certain stiffness, I've heard,
can affect the joints. Enough changes of loud plaid
clothing from Penney's or Goodwill.

> *This from a man who mows the lawn*
> *in black wingtips and a souvenir sombrero.*

Brightening up the walls should be no problem
with your gross—pun and repetition noted—
of Sears portraits of the grandchildren crookedly displayed.

> *Every one a gem, despite the photographer's*
> *incompetence and the corny painted clouds.*

Let's face it. You'd die (sorry) without your television
and swing records. We could probably spring
for a good oversized unit with four-corner sound.

> *Best music God ever made. Those guys could play!*
> *Nothing less than a 56-inch HDTV.*
> *What if I drop my glasses?*
> *And don't forget the satellite dish.*

I think that's about it, once we include your Bible,
back issues of *God's Word Today* and *Catholic Digest*,
seventeen rosaries, and crates of holy cards whose causes
you gave fifty cents to for so many years.

Once those are all wheeled into position
I think you'll be good to go. I know we will.

> *Like I said, your time's coming.*
> *I'll need every minute just to pray*
> *you off the hook. Get you past that little dog that*
> *guards the entrance before he*
> *gnaws you off at the ankles. He'll bark at*
> *you in hieroglyphics and say, "No, I'm*
> *sorry, she's having a Beefeater*
> *Lemonade, but if you will kindly wait . . ."*
> *Stoli would be ok, too. What are you waiting for?*
> *Preservative, you know. I think we'll skip the*
> *gauze strips. Would Ace bandages do?*

Dolls

Grandma buries her fists in the mud beneath
the raveling stream her baby dolls played in
all those years ago.

They dived and swam, slick ceramic heads and
hands, cotton bodies soaked and heavy. They
never laughed, cried, or drowned.

Grandma is lost but remembers
their bubble cheeks, pouting mouths,
cloth skin a sexless, perfect shield.

She sees them deep at the end
of her arms, their faces unperturbed, clouds
of water drifting by, held breath

a miracle beneath her tireless hand.

Witness

Grandma's green velour bathrobe, slung last
night around one cherry-knob bedpost,
becomes her attendant.

From the doorway, the bedpost is a head
caught with its features in shadow
from behind.

Its proportions match perfectly the
extreme small size of the robe she
now wears.

The knob fills to a peaked cowl
while the right-hand sleeve extends itself on
the bed.

The rest drapes perfectly, a kneeling
figure who looks intently toward
the pillows.

The hem falls over the faint outline of
her slippers, the effect of feet.
Her guardian never moves.

I grow superstitious lingering here
behind this kneeling figure, inclined to
kneel myself

to this form of shadows,
pray along with her for one more night free
of troubled dreaming.

Kissing the Dead in Sleep

Frail as paper, a net of smoke, A
face etched on water,

This kiss upon her cheek
Felt softer than the air

Between words, the sweep
Of an empty brush

Against an empty page

Detection Limit

*is the lowest quantity of a substance
that can be distinguished from the absence of that substance
(a blank value) within a stated confidence level*

Stakeout

It's so hard to gauge this job,
To stake out the night
Alone in a car at the corner, One
half-drawn Venetian blind To
watch blindly,

As if all the rest going down
Wouldn't distract a saint,
The city humming around you
Like a body and you the heart
With a badge over it Supposed
to pump and purify

Like some seedy movie dick
In a B-grade fedora
Who keeps reminding himself
'Motive. Think motive' Through
a three-day beard
Because this could be his big break

Instead of the real thing, Dull
and full of sleep,
The deed done somewhere else,
The blood dried already
On the hands or feet, The
ghost already steam From
a manhole

The facts nothing but rumor And
the witnesses lying low,
Unsavory truths at every turn
But the crux buried in dust.
A bit of ash, a stain,
A few mumbled words,
Who can tell?

And the cold by this time
Stiffening your arteries
And knees, until you wake up With
a start to curse and wonder
Who slipped town behind the blinds
While you were down.

A Thickened Plot

Too aware of the folded corpse
in the boot, I try the back roads of TV: a
classic British mystery.
My role foreshadows collapse.

Clarinet arpeggios
rise through leafless trees as smoke.
The narrow lane to Basingstoke
is dark with ancient echoes

beneath a scimitar of moon.
My severed head is on the fence,
my heart is thick with evidence.
I must confess to something soon.

Grey in his navy suit, the sleuth
takes contradiction for a spin
in his anonymous sedan.
He and Pilate only want the truth.

I see the Gothic country house
cut out against a louring sky.
What waits is merely destiny,
a small grey mouse.

It crawls inside the moldering walls,
omnivorous and dumb.
We barely hear his tiny thumbs
reclaim our fire-lit hall.

I am indifferent but to blame.
My tux is worn and stained.
The sideboard sherry has been drained and I
have had my dram.

Another body has been found on
the crumbling South Portico.
It has the same dry bullet hole behind
the face that lies face down.

Suspicion spreads like melting ice.
The butler and his wife lock
up the butter knives
and rinse the leaded crystal twice.

Sleet stings the cathedral panes
preliminarily, the snow
to follow builds its breath to blow oaks
and heirlooms to smithereens.

Night comes on again. We must stay
together and alone.
The sleuth has broken down in Scone. He
won't be any help today.

My bedroom fire, drafty and small,
gutters and cracks, the embers flare.
The storm screams. I sit and stare.
A small grey shadow climbs the walls.

It's come to this. Some decision crawls
toward its appointed hour. What I
wouldn't give for one more Whiskey
Sour—and revision.

In Situ

The forensic specialist took pains *in situ* all
day: exactly angled limbs, bent clues of
fabric, stain, the path of scavengers across
hands, forearms, face. Integers

flee across his laptop as arc lights burn night
away from all he will not learn
in time because truth dies, the yellow plastic
ribbon a cage for the quick and slow.

Patience calls both scholars of the gray places,
pollen grain and fingerprint, the busy factory of
decay moiling with quiet
energy, too slow for the host, too fast for the guest.

Each stares intently, but the dead man knows
what the doctor seeks. He keeps it close.
The doctor reads the signs. He will find his
way from the exit to the entry wound.

The routine gestation rate insects bring.
The rotting foot as it lovingly clings
to the trouser cuff. Nature will do
her best to melt the false from the true.

Whirling red lights, static crunch of radios,
blurring uniforms, cameras, crowds, and videos
have gone back into silence. He is alone beside
the library of bone.

Soon fluorescent light will steal
a ghostly blue from the stainless steel.
Identified, yet almost anonymous
at last, each sleeps inside his narrow house.

Near Kigali, 1995

We were in a kind of fog,
a fog of cruelty, he said, turning his scythe. That
sounds a television reason, I know,
but there is this difference—he lowered his head
toward the ground where we sat
just beyond the line of the others in blue scrubs
scraping their shovels and rakes. With my machete I
followed no script I recognized. I must
have believed some of the reasons I heard:
They were never quite human, they would kill
us if we did not kill them first,
they had chosen not to flee. Yet I knew
what I did, and that I did more even than
murder needed. I crushed children with
stones, held them
under water, sliced out a fetus
while its mother could still scream, chopped limb by
limb strong men because I could,
then watched them die by inches. And I know I
did all these things. I knew it then.
I was not crazy, though I know
I was not sane. I need the better word.

And it was not anger, not the anger I
knew all my life. Is there an anger
cold and deep as death itself, and as emotionless? I
want to say my right arm did these things,
my hard-muscled shoulder. I want to
accuse my targeting eyes, the metallic smells
of the blood my nose recognized, skin that knew
its tangible stickiness and spray, its beadlike dropping.
Each of these I know to be true and false.

Down these long rows my fellow prisoners
send their sickles and machetes singing
through the air. I imagine earth itself

flesh invaded, pulled apart. I remember.
We have no guards. We can walk away
any time. We do not have to be here.
We have chosen to plant ourselves here
in the impossible place and labor of forgiveness.

I do not think we can believe what we say,
but we believe we must say it. We must choose now
when it is too late for choice because
we have chosen, for now, to continue living
among the dead faces we have become, dearer
than any son or daughter,
wife or mother, the first of those whom we will see if
the stories are true, if across the last brown river we
will find all we saw and did and understand it for the
first time. I myself will not be
among the understood, though I pray still to
step onto the shore to find the death
that separates me from the past, that severs
for all time this articulate sorrowing
disbelieving shell from all it cannot deny,
forget, ignore, cut into infinitely small pieces
until they disappear, invisible as breath.

I am an arithmetic of actions,
a simple sum walking in baggy pants.
I recognize the call of the howler monkeys,
parrots, hyenas, but I cannot go.
My hands grip this long blade
and I clear weeds for new roads, for a school that
will fill with living faces, if any can be found.

I will visit them in my street clothes,
see in the empty desks before the doors open
those I alone bring with me. I will teach them from
the large desk all I know, and they will
listen with a grave seriousness no one can mimic. I
will teach them, chalk dust falling on my sleeves,

down the pleats of my trousers. Here,
I will say, here are the reasons you cannot live without
and came here in your uniforms each day
to find. Here, on the board, is the equation justified.
Do not drift or turn away. Stay with me.
It is necessary to be here together today, to
bend down above our books and papers,
cling to them as to the promises your mothers taught
you. They too will be waiting
for you. I pray to see you go to them.

Aubade

Just in time, another day
rescued by traffic and the blur of leaves shifting
sound into color through October light.

I catch winks of chrome,
spurs of glass pinched by sunlight
and thrown to memory still trailing echoes.

Leaves of ready color fall to coat
the earth I believe in, though
I cannot see the yard below the window.

As I believe in the tiny people
flying by, mannequins stiffly propped up or
flat black silhouettes painted on glass.

No two of anything is quite the same except
the gate I open for them
into the vacancy of nine o'clock.

Just in time. I was too weak
for proportion, the strain of supplying
depth, the manufacture of context:

hands warm around a leather-wrapped wheel,
a color dial of pin oak leaves around the birdfeeder,
other lives haunting the houses up the street,

a lawn below the plummeting leaves
receptive to decay and rebirth, the edifice
memory erects day after day to carry on

the vivid task of filling and surrounding
casement windows with a frame, crosshatch of
smaller panes, lenses of the everyday

I reduce to signal, delay, a beat faint
but steady. At last, a screen to act upon. Just
world enough to measure measurement

against, explain nothing away again
with everything.

www.ingramcontent.com/pod-product-compliance
Lightning Source LLC
Chambersburg PA
CBHW051050160426
43193CB00010B/1136